HACKING THE
COMMON CORE

HACKING THE COMMON CORE

10 Strategies for Amazing Learning in a Standardized World

Michael Fisher

x10
PUBLICATIONS

Hacking the Common Core
© 2016 by Times 10 Publications

These books are available at special discounts when purchased in quantity for use as premiums, promotions, fundraising, and educational use. For inquiries and details, contact us: mark@times10books.com.

Published by Times 10
Cleveland, OH
http://hacklearningseries.com

Cover Design by Tracey Henterly
Interior Design by Steven Plummer
Editing by Ruth Arseneault
Proofreading by Jennifer Jas

Library of Congress Control Number: 2015908743
ISBN: 978-0-9861049-2-3
First Printing: February, 2016

TABLE OF CONTENTS

ACKNOWLEDGEMENTS

MANY THANKS TO the members of the Hack Learning Facebook group. In particular, I'd like to thank Gerard Dawson and Christopher Reed, both of whom offered insightful feedback. All of the member comments made the manuscript better, and I sincerely appreciate your time and thoughtful contributions.

Yet again, I thank my family for their support as I spent nights and weekends on the computer, in the office, and at the coffee shop around the corner. Your patience is extraordinary.

Thank you to all of the schools and teachers in the "Hack in Action" sections. Your expertise and stories will help myriad others navigate their own practices. You are all exceptional and highly effective educators, and I value very much the opportunity to work with and learn from you.

Sincere thanks to the eagle-eyed Ruth Arseneault for her thoughtful edits and precise and insightful feedback. I always grow as a writer when I have opportunities for quality feedback from others.

Extra special thanks to Mark Barnes, visionary hacker extraordinaire, who saw an opportunity to bring some method to the madness of today's educational landscape. Hats off, friend. You are equal parts Jobs and Zuckerberg, and I sincerely appreciate the invitation to delve into this mindset.

This book is dedicated to all of the women in my family. My wife, my children, my mother, my sister, my aunts, mother-in-law and my grandmother are all phenomenal women. In one way or another they are all teachers, for they have taught me the most important lessons in my life. I love you all, and I thank you wholeheartedly.

PUBLISHER'S FOREWORD

As a teacher, author, and publisher, I have condemned most books about the Common Core Standards because I'm no fan of automating teaching and standardizing learning. Many of these books use the Common Core to homogenize learning and construct teachers as automatons. The Common Core exists, though, and while the standards are here guiding instruction, educators need more than do-this and do-that handbooks that offer little more than a prescription for test preparation. The Common Core needs to be hacked, and there's no one better for this task than CCSS expert Mike Fisher. Fisher debunks the mythology surrounding the standards and provides amazing strategies that will help you bring fun back to learning, even in our standardized world.

Hacking the Common Core is the fourth installment of the *Hack Learning Series*, a collection of books by outstanding teachers, speakers, and thought leaders. *Hack Learning* authors are all education hackers; that is, they strive to solve problems with right-now solutions that don't require that cliché for improvement, the five-year plan.

Education hackers seek solutions by exploring ideas wherever they find them, whether in or out of school, in the technology world or in the physical world. They are tinkerers and fixers. Like all hackers, they see solutions to problems that other people do not see. The label "hacker" originated in the field of technology, referring to those who circumvented or subverted systems to make innovations. Steve Jobs and Mark Zuckerberg might be considered technology's greatest hackers. No one taught them how to build an operating system or a social network, but they saw possibilities that others couldn't see.

The *Hack Learning Series* is a collection of books written by people who, like Jobs and Zuckerberg, see things through different lenses. They are specialists—the absolute best problem-solvers in their professions. They live to grapple with problems that need to be turned upside down and viewed from another perspective. The fix may appear unreasonable to those plagued by the issue, but to the hacker the solution is evident, and with a little hacking it will be as clear and beautiful as a gracefully designed smartphone or a powerful social network.

INSIDE THE BOOKS

Each book in the *Hack Learning Series* contains chapters, called Hacks, which are composed of these sections:

- **The Problem:** Something educators are currently wrestling with that doesn't yet have a clear-cut solution.

- **The Hack:** A brief description of the author's unique solution.

- **What You Can Do Tomorrow:** Ways you can take the basic hack and implement it right away in bare-bones form.

- **A Blueprint for Full Implementation:** A step-by-step system for building long-term capacity.

- **Overcoming Pushback:** A list of possible objections you might come up against in your attempt to implement this hack and how to overcome them.

- **The Hack in Action:** A snapshot of an educator or group of educators who have used this hack in their work and how they did it.

I am proud to be a contributing author and publisher of the *Hack Learning Series*, which is changing how we view and solve problems. When you finish reading this book, you will understand how to unravel the complexities of the Common Core. Better yet, you might see solutions to other problems that you've overlooked: This is Hack Learning. You might become a hacker. And that's a good thing.

—MARK BARNES, EDUCATION HACKER

AUTHOR'S NOTE

THIS BOOK IS unlike anything I've written before. As with all the books in the *Hack Learning Series*, each of the hacks follows a formula for implementation so that readers can easily identify elements that will be meaningful for them. It's analogous to a tool like Pinterest, where one can find unique and more efficient ways to tackle interesting projects. Even with a formulaic approach and anecdotal scenarios, this is not a "theory into practice" book. It is centered on best practices that are intended to help teachers gain insight and ideas; so it's more of a "practice informs better practice" book.

As a professional developer, I often weave several theoretical frameworks together for maximum impact when I work with schools. The same is true here. As such, in-text citations that would support theoretical evidence are not included in the traditional way. My professional decisions are guided by my predecessors, so where it is necessary, I incorporated the names of these educational experts and where (or how) their collective ideas informed my opinion about these hacks. It is my sincere hope that you will extend your own professional learning by further investigating the ideas by these important educators.

—MICHAEL FISHER

INTRODUCTION

Why the Common Core State Standards need to be hacked

THERE IS HARDLY a day that goes by when some aspect of the Common Core is not in the media. It's the source of the ills around teacher evaluation and new standardized assessments, and by extension it has become the catch-all for everything wrong with education in America. The Common Core continues to be a hot topic in 2016 even though it emerged back in 2010. I think it's still news after six years because teachers, administrators, and students are continuing to struggle with exactly what it is they should be doing. Align curriculum with college and career readiness or with a standardized test? Teach for transfer or for surface-level recall? Design curriculum or accept the advice of a textbook vendor? With so much information coming from multiple sources, what does one believe and how does one act on such an information overload?

The Common Core could benefit from a few successful work-arounds—tricks and strategies to make what we do more efficient, easier to understand, and ultimately more meaningful for our students. To effect this change, educators must consider what we know about higher student achievement and systemic change. Both require taking time and purposeful steps toward a goal. Regardless of the hopes some critics hold, there is no magic elixir to cure the ills of the Common Core. Nor will effecting wholesale changes effectively purge the system of ailments. Sick patients don't take all of the prescribed medicine at once. They take it little by little, getting better over time, until they've reached a healthy state. Otherwise, the overdose kills them.

Right now we are in overdose mode in most states around the country. We cherry-pick perceived best courses of action and then apply them all at once. Injecting the educational body with restorative doses of Race to the Top is hardly a good response to the diagnosed illnesses of the system, regardless of how many snake oil merchants flog it. I think we need a second opinion.

The ideas proposed in this book are not intended to be a universal remedy: They're more geared toward saving time, easing frustrations, and finding a balance between new initiatives and those effective procedures we already know. It's difficult for educators to habitually think in innovative ways when vendors and state education departments are constantly restricting us. Our students still need their teachers.

Since their rollout in 2010, the Common Core Standards have been widely vilified, thanks in part to minutiae that are usually only tangentially connected to the actual standards. That's a good thing in the sense that, in general, people's problems relate, not to the standards per se, but to issues associated with them, including new curricula, vendor products, assessments, and evaluations. The standards themselves are not wildly different from previous iterations of standards, in terms of the way sophistication of thinking develops from lower grade levels to upper grade levels. While they perhaps focus too narrowly on a few instructional necessities, the standards themselves are not evil, nor are they impossibly rigid; in fact, they are definitely malleable in execution.

The potential for flexibility in implementing the Common Core will be our learning zone in this book. We'll discuss where to find the malleability; where to upgrade and translate and be creative; where to apply what we know about good instruction, effective teaching, and common sense.

We teach students, not standards. The standards offer only grade-level benchmarks. They do not dictate curriculum. They do not dictate pacing. They do not dictate scaffolds or extensions or opportunities for personalization. If we separate the standards from the overblown discourse of fear that has been used to characterize them, we find they are just statements of expectations by grade level. When we ground our examination in the standards themselves, we can distance ourselves from the view that nothing about them is worth consideration. Likewise, we will not ally ourselves with those who would have educators blindly adopt any resource that is labeled "Common Core Aligned." Let's be realistic: While the standards are not the demonic manifestation of all that is wrong in the education system, neither are they perfect, nor infallible.

We have a vital responsibility to get education right: Students need us to prepare them for the world they live in now and the world they will inherit. Despite the shift in standards, the fundamentals of education have not changed. We still want to create lifelong learners and facilitate deeper thinking. What we know about good instruction can still happen with the Common Core, but we must be strategic about our instructional and standards-based curriculum decisions.

There's no time to waste. We've got some hacking to do.

SHIFT HAPPENS

Make sense of the umbrella view

*The only thing you sometimes have control over is
perspective. You don't have control over your situation.
But you have a choice about how you view it.*
—CHRIS PINE, ACTOR

THE PROBLEM: TEACHERS ARE OVERWHELMED
WITH NEW STANDARDS

TEACHERS CONTINUE TO be overwhelmed by the Common Core
Standards to the point of inaction. In many classrooms, this
has a rippling negative impact on assessments and teacher evalua-
tions. More often than not, the overwhelmed feeling stems from lack
of professional development and absence of professional conversa-
tions about what really matters when a teacher aligns practice to the
Common Core. This is especially true in subject areas apart from
English language arts and math, where alignment to the Common
Core sometimes consists of little more than labeling lesson plans
"Common Core Aligned" rather than prompting intentional acts of

thinking, analysis, vocabulary acquisition, and developing conceptual knowledge.

THE HACK: LOOK TO THE INSTRUCTIONAL SHIFTS

Take a step back and look at this confusion from a different perspective. Specifically, look to the instructional shifts, which define considerations for upgrading instructional practice across all subject areas and grade levels. You should also look to the College and Career Readiness (CCR) Capacities and the Standards for Mathematical Practice in the prefatory material included with each set of standards.

There are two sets of instructional shifts. In English language arts, these shifts include:

- Reading complex text and increasing a student's vocabulary

- Reading, Writing, and Speaking about evidence in both literary and informational texts

- Building knowledge through content-rich texts

In math, these shifts include:

- Focusing on fewer topics for the sake of conceptual understanding and greater depth

- Understanding the coherence between interconnected topics and thinking

- Rigorous pursuit of conceptual understanding, fluency, skills, and application

If we remove the sometimes overwhelming breadth of the standards from the curriculum conversations and instead focus only on the shifts, capacities, or practices, we can start moving toward intentional actions.

These intentional actions will not only move us into more contemporary teaching and learning, but will also be less overwhelming.

Beyond the instructional shifts lies another umbrella area under which alignment to the Common Core can occur: the CCR capacities and the math practices.

The CCR capacities, in general, ask that students build content knowledge, think independently and interdependently, attend to multiple types of audiences and tasks, value evidence, use technology strategically and capably, and engage a global perspective.

> **Every single standard in the Common Core relates back to these capacities and practices in some way.**

The math practices, in general, ask that students persevere in solving problems, look for patterns and reason abstractly, defend their thinking when solving problems and be able to critique the thinking of others, create mathematical models and use mathematical tools appropriately, look for structure, be precise, and look at their unique ways of solving problems to build speed and fluency.

Without having a week's worth of professional development about translating standards into instruction, just these few big ideas are usually enough to jump-start teachers' thinking around intentional actions that they can take in their classrooms immediately.

Every single standard in the Common Core relates back to these capacities and practices in some way. In fact, the Mastery Connect Common Core App specifically aligns each of the standards to one or more of these capacities or practices, if you'd like to have "in your hand" access to these alignments.

WHAT YOU CAN DO TOMORROW

While it will still involve some brief reading, this hack can actually be implemented fairly quickly. Full articulation and alignment to standards can come later, but for now, consider some of the following:

- **Access and read.** Find the Instructional Shifts, the College and Career Readiness Capacities, and/or the Standards for Mathematical Practice at *CoreStandards.org* or *AchievetheCore.org*.

- **Set a purpose for understanding.** As you read through these brief descriptions, read with a purpose. I like to use the "See, Think, and Wonder" visible thinking routine from *Harvard's Project Zero*. "See" by noting what jumps out at you as important information; when you "Think," make connections between what you're reading and other ideas that are similar; to "Wonder," ask questions that you have as a result of reading the text.

- **Think of intentional actions.** Whatever important ideas you pulled out or connections you made while you read form your new action zone. They will become your primary jumping-off points as you engage this hack and create an action plan for upgrading your professional practice.

- **Choose one new thing from the capacities or practices and just do it.** Ask students why they are thinking what they're thinking. Make models, ask questions, or talk to students about being perseverant. Consider the capacities and practices as a menu of options to upgrade facets of your current curriculum.

A BLUEPRINT FOR FULL IMPLEMENTATION

Step 1: Set a goal for future upgrades.

Determine what you want to do or accomplish. What ideas interested you or connected to other ideas as you read through the capacities, practices, or instructional shifts? Perhaps you saw a through-line around "thinking" and your goal is to have students defend their thinking or their choices of tools and resources during the learning process. Perhaps you discovered something from the capacities and practices "menu" that is worth applying across other units or sharing with colleagues. Consider essential goals and how you would ultimately determine what's worth upgrading. If you need criteria for determining what's worthy here, look at the upgrades through this single lens: Is what I'm doing what is best for kids?

Step 2: Create an action plan.

Note what actions you must take to make your goal happen. Consider what you need to change in your practice to meet your goal. In the case of upgrading your practice around "thinking strategies," perhaps your action includes tweaking current lesson plans to define and document how you ask questions of students and how you encourage them to ask questions of each other, holding them accountable for evidence from learning materials to explain their thinking. You may add protocols or rubrics that define, and encourage higher-order questions that require students to apply, analyze, and evaluate. Additionally, you may seek to extend your efforts around student thinking by ditching rote activities such as memorization or worksheets and instead opting for authentic opportunities that involve inquiry, research, and project-based learning.

Step 3: Define your intended success.

Decide how you will know that you have met your goal. Determine what concrete evidence or artifact will show that you've accomplished what you set out to do. Perhaps you will have developed new habits, methodologies, or assessment products that you documented in your curriculum materials. Perhaps you will have invited students into the conversation about preferred ways to engage in thinking activities.

Step 4: Talk to your colleagues.

Discuss your upgrade with your colleagues. Ask them about capacities, practices, and instructional shifts they've engaged in their classrooms. They may give you new ideas that prompt you to fine-tune your action plan or adjust your ideas about what success looks like. If you are planning thinking skills and strategies, seek out those colleagues who already engage their students in evidence-based discussions and writing practices. Perhaps make an effort to do some peer observations of your colleagues engaging in these practices.

Step 5: Do the actions and reflect.

Follow your action plan and see what happens. Document your intentions for your plans, units, or map. Then, implement these actions, discussions, research opportunities, or projects with students. Reflect on what happened during the learning moments and after the learning moments. Did you achieve the desired depth? Did students seem to be digging deeper than they have in the past? Did the ideas work, or do they need to be adjusted based on student performance, interest, or engagement?

Step 6: Spiral to the next goal.

Blueprints for improvement are often characterized as cycles in which one action continues to completion and then a new cycle begins with a different action. That's not how this blueprint functions. As you continue to improve your professional practice, you learn what works and what doesn't. When you're ready to move on, don't go back to the drawing board—enhance the existing blueprint by using what you've learned to spiral upwards into increasingly better work.

OVERCOMING PUSHBACK

My administrator requires Common Core Standards alignment in my plans. Before you lose sleep about this, remember that I mentioned that the capacities, practices, and shifts align to a variety of standards. Find an area of interest, importance, or connection, then look for the standards that align to it. This way, you will be able to show alignment by tracing your focus area across standards as you plan your lessons. It may also help to discuss your intentions with an English language arts teacher or math teacher who can quickly tell you which grade-specific standards are associated with the focus area.

I teach art or music or physical education: How do the CCSS apply to me? Besides giving opportunities for authentic vocabulary instruction with domain (content) specific vocabulary or developing critical thinking about processes specific to your content area, be mindful of the depth of instruction. Many aspects of these three subject areas are opportunities for analysis: Explore how music is received by the listener, examine connections in music between pop culture and historically significant happenings, analyze artists' intentions or choices, study procedures for improving sports performance, etc. You might look back to Bloom's Taxonomy to invite higher-order thinking like application, analysis, evaluation, and creation. Any action that involves greater depth often involves better discussions, evidence-based thinking, inquiry, and stronger vocabulary development, both in speaking and writing. All of these outcomes align with capacities, practices, and shifts, which in turn align with individual Common Core Standards. Also note that there are specific standards in grades 6-12 for literacy in history, science, and technical subjects. They are banded by grade levels (6-8, 9-10, 11-12) and are generally easier to read and implement than those in the English language arts literacy document. There is no directive that teachers outside of ELA or math must align to every standard. Here, a group effort for full alignment makes better sense. Consider what standards might naturally fit with physical education. Art, music, and other courses may also find natural alignments. Together, all of these classes cover the breadth of standards without any one course being obliged to cover them all.

THE HACK IN ACTION

Two years prior to the statewide implementation of the Common Core Standards, a K-8 private school in Southern Georgia began a curriculum mapping initiative to document a student's journey through its system. Teachers had frequent professional development on learning about the curriculum mapping process and the technology application they would use to record their work.

The teachers embarked on this initiative with the goal of having a map, without necessarily realizing the amount of discussion, collaboration, consensus, and documentation it would take. They worked hard, and after two years did indeed produce a draft of a year-long curriculum map for each grade level. Then, the tired teachers at this school learned that the rest of the state's public schools had just agreed to align to the Common Core under the Race to the Top transition. It was exhausting for them to think of redoing and realigning all of the work that they had done.

This district decided to explore the instructional shifts as a first step toward Common Core alignment. Their online mapping program had a box reserved for reflection, so they made a collective decision to use it to document how the instructional shifts were apparent, either in their current instruction or in their ideas for implementing the shift into their units of study.

These teachers participated in professional development around the shifts (this included conversations about the capacities and practices as well, but these weren't the focal point of their work), specifically looking at delineating potential roles for teachers and students to fulfill during each shift. The administration gave them work time over the first semester of the school year to record the shifts in their maps, and encouraged them to read their grade-specific standards to familiarize themselves with the language.

In the spring semester, the company that housed their mapping system and their curriculum maps added all of the Common Core Standards to the system. Teachers could now extend their records around the instructional shifts and attach individual grade-specific standards to their documented units using the software's drop-down menus. This created opportunities for further map upgrades that considered the language of the Common Core Standards, alignment to skills, alignment to deeper cognitive opportunities, and eventually, using what they've documented to grow the system and their efforts around creating and maintaining a more contemporary curriculum.

Beginning the work from a less imposing starting point using the instructional shifts or the capacities and practices actually helps to create a deeper level of buy-in and understanding about what teachers are responsible for when they align their work to the Common Core Standards. This allows teachers to approach the transition gradually rather than having standards dumped in their laps. It also allows for a specific way to keep previously documented curriculum alive as they upgrade their work one thing at a time, making the work less overwhelming and ultimately more productive.

CLOSE IN ON CLOSE READING

Navigate a destructive misinterpretation of the standards

The single biggest problem in communication is the illusion that it has taken place.
—GEORGE BERNARD SHAW, PLAYWRIGHT

THE PROBLEM: CLOSE READING HAS BEEN MISINTERPRETED

CHIEF AMONG SEVERAL misconceptions about implementing Common Core Standards is insistence on close reading virtually every text a student encounters. This particular misconception translates into skewed instructional practice, leading students (and teachers) toward more opportunities for frustration than for deep learning. Vendors compound this frustration by creating curriculum products that focus on a narrow band of standards, promote daily practice with overused and nonvariant methodologies, and present assessments that measure what's easy but not what matters. In short, close reading isn't really what some curriculum designers, particularly vendors, purport it to be. It's a misinterpretation at best, and a quick way to kill the love of reading at worst.

THE HACK: CLOSE IN ON WHAT THE STANDARD ACTUALLY SAYS

The hack, in this case, is two-fold. First, you need to know what the Common Core actually says about close reading, and second, you need to use this knowledge to appraise and adapt your current curriculum, particularly if it is a vendor product that you did not have a hand in designing.

For many of the schools I work in around the United States, aligning to the Common Core Standards involved the adoption of a new Common Core aligned text or resource, a pat on the back, and a good luck wave as the teacher walked down the hall. Few schools based changes on conversations about curricular impact, what the standards actually require students to know and be able to do, or how to be pro-active and ready for a school's specific population of students.

In the interest of being well informed, the first part of this hack will describe exactly what the Common Core Standards communicate about close reading.

The Common Core document refers to close reading only in its anchor standards, which are the K-12 umbrella versions of the grade-specific standards. The very first anchor standard in literacy states:

> Read closely to determine what the text says explicitly and to make logical inferences from it; cite specific textual evidence when writing or speaking to support conclusions drawn from the text.

This standard has taken on a life of its own based on the first two words: "Read closely." As the International Literacy Association has pointed out in its annual update of trends in literacy education, "What's Hot, What's Not," close reading is "Hot."

Look at the context to clarify the relationship of the words "read closely" to the remaining words in this anchor's standard. When these two words are separated from the remaining 29 words, other necessary skills are more distinctly apparent:

> **To clarify, close reading is not mentioned again in any grade-specific standard.**

- determine what the text says explicitly,

- make logical inferences,

- cite textual evidence,

- support conclusions.

Reading closely, or close reading as it is now known, is merely a title given to the suite of skills associated with the analysis of text to ensure that students achieve the standard's purpose. To use an analogy, close reading serves as a sort of magnifying glass through which the reader can view a text's attributes in minute detail. This detailed magnification deepens students' understanding of the text so they may develop the anchor standard's learning expectations. Using the magnifying glass is not a skill to be learned, it is just a lens through which students can address this standard's priorities. This standard is the only place in the Common Core Standards where "read closely" is even mentioned. To clarify, close reading is not mentioned again in any grade-specific standard.

Doesn't that make you wonder why virtually all vendors or commercial curriculum developers focus so deeply on close reading? The act of analyzing text is meant to be a deep-thinking activity, though not the only activity that a teacher has students participate in. Multiple types of interactions with texts are necessary for students to become better readers and writers. When deciding what to close read, note that some texts are more worthy of analysis than others. Focusing on one skill, such as close reading, pretty much guarantees that students will hate reading.

The second part of this hack involves appraising and adapting your curriculum. It's time to do some pruning and cut out parts that are overused, frustrating, cumbersome, and boring. You can revise your curriculum regardless of whether you are using a vendor product or a locally created document. You know your students better than the vendor does. It's time to put professional practice ahead of professional products.

WHAT YOU CAN DO TOMORROW

- **Resist the urge to analyze the text.** If you are planning on close reading a particular text with your students tomorrow, ditch that lesson plan. Instead, have students connect the text with other texts or media. Brainstorming connections creates mental Velcro for students to remember what they experience at school. Give them memorable experiences.

- **Don't close read every text.** Instead, look for opportunities to address the standard's skills directly. Help students to sequence information, such as one might do in a multi-step word problem in math. You might discuss the ways settings, characters, and figurative language advance the plot or draw the reader into the story more deeply, and have students provide evidence from the text to support their thinking. Look to the associated analysis skills that are embedded in this standard rather than focusing on close reading. Each of the associated skills is important to meeting the standard. There is no linear order to teaching them to students, though the standards imply that one should teach them all at some point.

- **Let your essential question be, "How can I help my students be better readers and writers?"** Don't worry about the language of the standards so much as you worry about improving the reading comprehension of all students by exposing them to multiple texts and opportunities to read voraciously at school.

A BLUEPRINT FOR FULL IMPLEMENTATION

Step 1: Take a critical look at your curriculum.

Whether you are using a vendor product or not, you need to appraise your instructional practices. Do your plans reflect daily or frequent opportunities for reading closely? When you read closely with students, do you always use a standard procedure, either one dictated by a vendor product or a habit you've gotten into? Cut a significant portion of any close reading out of your plans. I'm not suggesting you eliminate analysis, just stop whatever it is you're doing that you're calling close reading, particularly if a vendor dictates your definition of close reading. Trust me, the students are tired of it. Productive analysis can take many forms, including asking and answering text-dependent questions, annotating, providing evidence of an author's purpose, defending one's thinking, and connecting ideas across multiple texts.

Step 2: Make close reading an occasional activity rather than a classroom staple.

While some text analysis is necessary, teachers should focus more on helping students determine main ideas, create summaries, ask and answer questions, use evidence to support thinking, and understand contextual vocabulary. Document your lesson and unit intentions for developing good comprehension skills, and explain how you will teach those skills. Look to the language of the grade-specific standards, paying particular attention to the verbs, which will indicate what actions students must be able to do. Just don't let close reading or text analysis be an everyday action. Literacy in the classroom should never be *only* about comprehension. Balance is necessary here. Read to build background. Read for the love of doing so. Then, when important, or as designed, analyze the text for deeper meaning.

Step 3: Ensure that students frequently explain their thinking.

Students should be explaining their thinking, explaining why they think X occurred, explaining how they drew a particular conclusion, explaining how X affects Y. They should be defending, rationalizing, supporting, or expounding on their ideas as often as they can, both orally and in writing and other ways of representing, perhaps even by creating a digital presentation or artwork.

Step 4: Collaborate with your colleagues.

Facilitate a consensus about what text analysis means, emphasizing the decision not to closely read everything. Brainstorm a list of ways to meet outcomes that do not necessarily entail close reading so that everyone has options.

Ensure that administrators are part of this discussion, and help them understand that as learning leaders they should base decisions on their own knowledge of your particular population of students rather than blindly trusting a vendor who does not know them.

Step 5: Examine any state assessments that your students take.

Most states that have standardized testing will publish some sort of testing manual or guide before the actual assessment. In many cases, this includes either a test map or a statement about standards alignment. Pay close attention to whether this emphasizes only the close reading standard (Standard 1 for both literary and informational texts). If it incorporates numerous standards, adjust lesson and unit planning accordingly.

OVERCOMING PUSHBACK

Our district requires us to use curriculum products verbatim and without deviation. What I'm proposing here applies specifically to close reading, but it should be extended to any methodology or vendor product. If you want to use Common Core effectively, I don't suggest that you *could* make these changes; I suggest that you *must* make these changes. In curriculum meetings with your colleagues and administrators, question adherence to the product and present data to support your statements. For instance, if students read closely every day and your common formative or benchmark assessments show them to be underperforming, particularly on skills associated with standards beyond the close reading standard, then suggest that as effective educators you should use that data to inform and redesign instructional practice. Students need a range of classroom experiences to become proficient readers.

I wasn't trained in literacy or English language arts but am still expected to do close readings with students. Regardless of your subject, close reading in your classroom doesn't have to follow a prescribed set of steps. Remember that the standard stipulates that students determine what the text says explicitly, make logical inferences, cite textual evidence, and support conclusions. Addressing this standard could be as simple as asking students to give reasons for their thinking. Have them point out which specific words help them draw conclusions about a character or situation, or question them about how tables, charts, and illustrations help them understand the text. Annotating text is also an act of close reading—students should pull out details, highlight information, and make connections within a text, all actions that support the development of comprehension skills. In music or art classes the text might be a musical composition or a painting or a sculpture. Think about what close listening or close viewing might look like across multiple types of media. All of this analysis involves close reading.

This isn't the way I've always done it. I hear this more often than you might think. There are some teachers who planned their lessons years ago and are unlikely to deviate from their original plan, nor have they any interest in designing something new. They see their practices as tried and true and feel it's up to the students to accommodate themselves to the teacher's perspective rather than it being the teacher's responsibility to appeal to the students. To combat entrenched close reading, start with invitation. Invite these teachers to see innovative practices and share success stories and bright spots around the school. Give them ideas that are easy to try and follow up with reflective conversations about their impact on students. Make sure these teachers feel like part of the team rather than dinosaurs who must be punished with the new standards.

THE HACK IN ACTION

When all of this hullabaloo around close reading started, I admit that when we read books at home with our six-year-old we began to explore their main ideas, determine their gist, and re-read selections to support the main idea with text-dependent questions. I would try strategies out on her that I was going to use with teachers in workshops, but she caught on to me quickly.

She became wary of reading with me, telling me that she would do so, but only if I didn't "test" her. Close, analytical reading at home turned into disruptive comprehension: We overused reading strategies to the point that it didn't help my daughter be a better reader; it hindered her progress. The fact that I, an experienced educator, discovered disruptive comprehension from a six-year-old floored me. A child could see it; why couldn't I?

We ultimately shifted to emphasize text-dependent questions developed in the moment and focus on important details rather than the overall main idea. I rarely disrupt her reading to drill her with a bunch of questions anymore, waiting until we have finished a story or a book to ask questions that would require going back to a particular page and providing specific evidence of her thought processes. Often, it is just a question or two, which seems to resonate more than the close reading I was forcing her to participate in.

I would like to note, though, that we have extended this version of analysis balanced with joy into her writing as well. She thinks of story ideas and the main message she wants to get across, brainstorms the details and then writes. Often the stories involve the same revolving cast of characters (ponies, princesses, and SpongeBob SquarePants). Our discussions about details in her writing are helping her to be a better reader as well.

I don't ask her questions about everything she reads. I want her to read purely for the fun of it or because she is interested in a particular topic sometimes. We get better at the things we do with regularity, practicing toward mastery, not because we learn sets of isolated skills and expect those skills to magically connect when it is time to perform. We aim to have students become proficient at the overarching goal, which in this case is becoming a fluent lifelong reader, not just an analytical reader.

The key here is that my daughter is reading and we are navigating both skills and processes together while she is reading. Sometimes the reading is more guided in nature, presenting opportunities to discuss improvement areas. Sometimes she reads to me so that I can hear what she is doing. Sometimes I still read to her, not so much anymore because I want her to hear me being a fluent reader, but just because she still lets me.

I hope that lasts for a little while longer.

Close reading concerns analysis of texts rather than being a discrete skill. The main literacy action students should be taking is simply to read as much and as often as possible. When appropriate, analyze the text in ways that support the language and intention of the standards: infer, draw conclusions, and understand author's purpose and craft and structure. Don't take a vendor's word for what close reading entails. Make strategic decisions about how you and your colleagues interpret the standards.

HACK 3

FRIDAY EVERY DAY

Formative assessment and brain-based strategies

*Neither comprehension nor learning can take
place in an atmosphere of anxiety.*
—ROSE KENNEDY, MATRIARCH

THE PROBLEM: TOO MUCH TO COVER

TEACHERS AND STUDENTS often share how frustrated they are
with the amount of information that classes cover since the new
standards came into play. Because of high stakes testing and teacher
evaluations, there is constant focus on running a race, perhaps to the
top, but not well. When we cover the curriculum in this way, it's like
noticing a kid's shoelaces are untied and rather than having him stop
to tie them, forcing him to run even faster down the track, ignoring
the tripping and slipping. Covering more, faster, is not the way to
improve performance.

Teachers don't feel like they have time to "uncover," to go deeply
into the learning and bring engagement and risk-taking back into
their professional practice. Teachers are asking the essential question,

"How can I cover the curriculum while aligning to standards and still be engaging and creative?"

THE HACK: BRING THE DELIGHTFULNESS OF FRIDAY TO EVERY DAY

I've been in hundreds of classrooms over the years and one of the observations I've made is that Friday is always better than Monday. Sure, in some classes, Fridays are testing days (stop doing that regularly, by the way), but more often than not, Fridays are more fun and engaging, perhaps with culminating activities like project presentations or fun activities that allow for practice or more informal, although still important, assessments.

> **"Friday is always better than Monday."**

Bring the happiness associated with Friday to every day of the week. In previous books, I've written about how engagement leads to high levels of learning and the creation of mental Velcro. We want the learning to stick. This is "Brain-Based Learning 101," where we intentionally create emotional connections through a variety of engagement strategies to affect student learning positively. It's *so* 1985, but it's also *so* contemporary. Some instructional strategies are both timely and timeless. Let's not lose what we know to be effective because its age makes it seem passé, or because of potentially overwhelming minutiae centered on the Common Core Standards.

WHAT YOU CAN DO TOMORROW

- **Analyze your Friday plans.** Figure out what is different about your Friday classes. Perhaps you offer students more opportunities for catching up on learning. Perhaps games and fun activities connect with the week's new learning. Perhaps you are more likely to schedule low-stress formative assessments. If Fridays are not your thing, then which days of the week do your students find more inspirational and engaging? Figure out what you do on the days when your students perceive you as engaging.

- **Apply your observations to other days of the week.** Whatever you learned in your analysis of your Friday or other engaging day, consider how you can apply the same planning and thinking to other, less engaging days. Get your plan book out or open up your online planning software and commit to making changes to your documented curriculum.

- **Stop worrying about timing and focus on learning.** The Common Core Standards help teachers navigate what students need to know and be able to do on their paths to college and career readiness. They are not a curriculum nor are they a prescriptive map for how we navigate the Common Core neighborhood. Any time we take up in superficially covering the standards disrupts the potential deep learning that could be happening. Focus on the learning. Focus on standards that have analogues and partners across their respective standards sets. (See Hack 6: Prioritize.) Look for those standards that are priorities because they develop conceptual knowledge that students will use now, in other classes, and for the rest of their lives. The other standards then become supporting in nature, helping teachers make informed decisions about what they teach. Don't let any vendor product determine these priorities.

A BLUEPRINT FOR FULL IMPLEMENTATION

Step 1: Find the Velcro.

Think back to a special trip you took as a child. Maybe you went to Disney World or sailed the River Thames. Maybe you visited the Acropolis or saw live kangaroos in Australia. Even now, these many years later, you could probably write a detailed account of the trip, complete with particulars about who you were with, what you did, maybe even what you ate. Now think back to September 26, 1992. Unless you were doing something out of the ordinary or the day is an anniversary or birthday, you probably don't remember much. The contrast between these two memories has to do with novelty. That which is different is memorable. Do you remember the worksheets you did in school or the field trips you took? My point here is: That which is different sticks. Experiencing the different provides an emotional attachment to the learning that the same old day in, day out routines do not. If you want to create mental Velcro, then look to find the fun, novel, awesome, and cool things in your curriculum, and do more of them.

Step 2: Make some critical cuts.

The best hacking one can do when overwhelmed with covering the curriculum is to metaphorically hack away at your plan. If you're using a vendor product, look for overlapping lessons, coinciding methodologies, anything that is repeated, and consider those prime possibilities for elimination. Then delete them without regret. Own your position as learning leader of your classroom. As a colleague, Marie Alcock, says, "We must be loyal to learning and defenders of innovation." If you're always teaching someone else's plan, how does that happen?

Step 3: Relieve your students' anxiety.

Teachers who are in the groove of covering the curriculum often have students who I refer to as "floaters." They aren't necessarily drowning, but they aren't moving with the current either. They hold themselves just enough above the water to survive. Remember that you are teaching children and not standards. If they are anxious, then the first responsibility of an effective educator is to lessen the anxiety by getting to the heart of the objective rather than skimming over the entire curriculum content or span of the standards.

Step 4: Worry more about the *how* and the *why* than the *what.*

The Common Core can be boiled down to one word: thinking. The most significant shift in the Common Core involves teaching conceptual-level knowledge rather than rote remembering of facts. The *what* of subject matter doesn't matter so much as the *how* and *why* of critical thinking. Rather than constantly building background knowledge, we need to shift our collective methodologies into zones of discovery and exploration.

Step 5: Think about the information your formative assessments provide.

Every teacher should make formative assessment central to the work of the classroom rather than aiming everything toward summative assessments. Be mindful of how students demonstrate mastery and quality as they work, and consider whether summative assessments even matter in terms of traditional objective assessments. Summative assessments that present opportunities for project- or problem-based assessment offer a teacher deeper understanding of what students know or are able to do. Formative assessments give opportunities not only for engaging mental Velcro, but also for shaping the intended demonstration of learning. Starr Sackstein covers this in greater depth in her book, *Hacking Assessment: 10 Ways to Go Gradeless in a Traditional Grades School.*

OVERCOMING PUSHBACK

I work on a grade-level team and not everyone is on the same page.
Converse. Collaborate. Commit. One central complication in the

Common Core rollout is that the whole educational system is teeming with variation. When I work in schools that operate in isolated zones, it's common to find that assessment data varies wildly, even among similar grade levels and content areas. If teachers don't have an understanding of their own niche and how they are situated within their curriculum community, then the educational ecosystem is in trouble and the teachers are endangered. And so are their students.

Two elements that vary significantly between classrooms are content and assessment. What looks like teaching is often more akin to assigning tasks, neglecting support for differentiated instruction or divergent thinking. It's the one-size-fits-all, linear version of teaching that was popular in the 19th century but has no place in this century. A purchased curriculum isn't going to change things either. Using basal readers, depending on any one resource, mandating teachers to be on the same page of the workbook on the same day, or making stakeholders controlled game pieces as opposed to valued contributors are all going to lead to failure, regardless of standards.

Teachers need to talk to each other, to their students, to their administrators. Administrators need to lead with inspiration rather than fear, and create what Janet Hale calls the "Aspen Grove Mentality," where stakeholders form an interrelated ecosystem of success. If all stakeholders can agree to some critical pieces so equity gets built into instruction, the intended curriculum will be in reach—because we designed it that way.

The last thing I have time for is re-planning my lessons. Time, or rather the lack of it, is the single common denominator for all teachers. Even if we could convince Mother Nature to add a couple of hours to each day, it probably still would not be enough. That said, if we're looking to engage students and have them perform better than ever before, then we really can't wait one more minute to start implementing changes. Realize that good planning up front actually saves you time on the back end. Deciding on specific and measurable objectives with a menu of student choice options to get there is a good start. So is ditching traditional notions about lesson planning. You don't need a daily six-point lesson plan to guide your work; you need an overall map, the details of which are as specific as you need them to be. Second, you should leverage your colleagues. If you're working with people who teach the same content and grade level, plan with them so everybody shares the load.

Our students are doing just fine, thank you very much. That's great, really it is, but aren't there always opportunities to move students further? I often challenge teachers to teach beyond the assessments for the sake of readiness and endurance and sophistication, as students grow older. Teach so that students are ready for any assessment. I once heard Andrew Chen, president of Edutron Corporation and former physics professor at MIT, make a transformational statement about one of the biggest differences in schools in the United States compared to those in other countries: "In most other countries in the world, the standards are the floor. In the United States, the standards are the ceiling." Consider the implications of this declaration. If the standards really should be where we start, then there certainly seems to be some room to improve.

THE HACK IN ACTION

Implementation of the Common Core in New York State was not exactly the smoothest of transitions. It still is in a precarious spot as teachers try to balance their own values around curriculum design with new assessments, state-supported vendor products, and teacher evaluations that are the opposite of logical.

A mid-state, seventh grade social studies team I worked with struggled during the first year, as they were implementing Common Core literacy standards on top of their current New York State history standards. The analytical reading and writing that the literacy standards for history and social studies demanded was already in their wheelhouse but in a "way we've always done it" mode. They were seeking to make the learning more accessible to contemporary students while maintaining alignment to the standards.

The team discussed what was of high interest in their classrooms, practices they wanted to try, and tools that were worth exploring. They wanted to continue to build background knowledge about historical happenings, but they wanted to do so in enriching and sophisticated ways that invited more opportunities for inquiry learning.

This school had created and maintained curriculum maps over the years, so after their discussion, this teaching team went back to the documented curriculum and began looking at alternatives in methodology and assessment. In particular, they invited more opportunities for comparative analysis of how past events were playing out in current events. They also considered changing some of their formative and summative assessments to digital demonstrations. These would require the same evidence-based writing that students used to do, but the work would now be project-based learning that culminated with multimedia presentations.

Bringing the wonder and joy of learning back into the picture matters very much, particularly for this generation of students. Covering the standards just to get through them doesn't really transfer learning; it just turns students off. We must apply the engaging aspects of our teaching to practices that aren't so engaging to facilitate changes in student performance and learning.

HACK 4

MORECABULARY

Create a new culture of vocabulary acquisition

The most important thing is to read as much as you can, like I did. It will give you an understanding of what makes good writing and it will enlarge your vocabulary.
—J. K. ROWLING, AUTHOR

THE PROBLEM: OUTDATED VOCABULARY INSTRUCTION

TRADITIONAL METHODS OF teaching vocabulary still pervade classrooms despite plentiful current research about word acquisition and process-oriented approaches. The field is full of respected educational researchers and leaders, including Robert Marzano, Marilee Sprenger, Janet Allen, Isabel Beck, Margaret McKeown, Irene Fountas, and Gay Su Pinnell, all supporting the same stance: Vocabulary acquisition is a process, not a rote task.

Lists of vocabulary words to be learned "just in case" and associated busywork activities, such as writing dictionary definitions and copying words multiple times, do not work. Testing vocabulary every Friday does not work. We're fifteen years into the 21st century and we're still preparing kids to enhance their vocabularies with methods popular in the 1950s. Come on. It's time to put this tradition to rest.

THE HACK: INTEGRATE A PROCESS APPROACH

Pronounce. Engage. Assess.

That's it. Just those three things. Pronouncing new words for students is essential for speaking fluency. Engaging with the words in multiple ways helps students retain the newly taught words, and ongoing assessment (not tests) is necessary to gauge students' levels of retention. Whatever vocabulary you are teaching explicitly, whether teacher- or student-selected, make sure those three actions are happening. Vocabulary instruction in the classroom isn't an event. It's a habit, perhaps even a culture. This is true for vocabulary words, sight words, academic words, domain-specific words, any words. Except for extremely specific, high-level content terminology, there are no grade boundaries for word acquisition. There may be grade-level recommendations for assessing vocabulary, particularly in writing, but our concern here is not assessment; it's receptivity. For students to master a powerful vocabulary, it's essential that they be exposed to lots and lots of words from a very early age.

Effective vocabulary instruction is a gift.

With regard to vocabulary acquisition, access equals success, and the earlier that access occurs, the better. Students should have receptive experiences with words very early on, even though the expressive level happens later. For instance, it's perfectly acceptable for a 4-year-old to use the word "nonconformity" and know what it means, even if she has yet to understand how letters make words. (Google "Marzano vs. a Four Year Old" if you want to see a video of this happening.)

The Common Core is full of standards that support vocabulary acquisition and meaning making, including Reading Standard 4 and all of the language standards. There are implications for the speaking and listening standards, too, as students need to both hear and orally use new words before they express them in writing. Vocabulary is the crux of one of the instructional shifts, so the more extensive vocabulary students develop when they are young, the more doors open for them into sophisticated texts and media experiences as they grow older. Effective vocabulary instruction is a gift.

WHAT YOU CAN DO TOMORROW

- **Stop having students do dictionary work.** Dictionaries, both traditional print behemoths and their digital ilk, should now be considered last resorts for transfer of meaning, unless the reader is comprehending at a level that leaving a text to discover a word's meaning will not derail their comprehension when they return to the text. Because of the number of words in our language, dictionary definitions are efficient, short records of a word's meaning, and as such are not accessible to students in a way that transfers understanding. Engage students by going beyond the dictionary. Have your class look for context clues, ask others for help, break words apart, explore etymology, think about word families, relate unknown words to familiar ones to bridge understanding, visualize or dramatize words, create games with new words. The list of possibilities is unlimited.

- **Stop testing vocabulary lists on Friday.** Friday is not the only day that vocabulary is important, though you'd never guess that was the case in many classrooms, even in 2016. This practice is still pervasive and it must stop. Vocabulary is important every day. We don't want students to associate knowing vocabulary only with getting through a test on Friday. This habituation virtually guarantees that they will forget all that they've learned. They cram on Thursday nights to perform well on Friday's quiz or test and then they push it right out of their minds, making room in their short-term memory for next week's words. What we do want is frequent formative assessment to integrate words into long-term memory through repeated contextual use.

- **Be sure to pronounce every new word.** In 2013, I had the great fortune to hear Maya Angelou speak. She's a storyteller, an amazing storyteller, and I sat in rapt attention to her tales. One of her anecdotes involved playing Monopoly with her brother Bailey on her kitchen floor. She emphasized the first three syllables, each with a long "o" sound (Moh-noh-poh-ly). She didn't know how it was supposed to sound until she was 11 or 12 years old and someone told her the correct pronunciation. Her story made me wonder how often students deal with that same scenario, hence the invitation above for teachers to pronounce every word for their students.

- **Practice using new words.** Multiple experiences with new words gives them staying power in a student's brain. Use the vocabulary you want your students to acquire. If you speak it, the students will speak it. Insist that students use the new words when speaking to you or each other. Likewise, create opportunities for students to use their new words often in writing. When conferring with them or offering feedback, question their word choices, focusing on those they are currently learning. Frequent formative assessment will help make new words permanent.

A BLUEPRINT FOR FULL IMPLEMENTATION

Step 1: Engage with words in multiple ways.

Every single one of the researchers I name-dropped in the problem section advocates for engaging experiences with vocabulary that include explanations, examples, elaborations, and extensions. Make these tasks part of every vocabulary acquisition moment and lesson. Have students explain new words and meanings orally and then transition their newly learned vocabulary to their writing, as they are ready to do so. Ask them to provide examples, such as visualizations and dramatizations. Encourage learners to elaborate on meanings by making connections to other related words like synonyms, particularly when writing, so that they don't habitually use the same limited number of words. Give opportunities to extend meanings by letting students create original stories or design a game using their new words. Teachers may also want to consider etymological analysis or multiple texts that involve the new words.

Step 2: Tell stories about words.

The human brain is hard-wired to learn from narrative. Teachers should share stories about words, particularly when introducing new words to students, and especially when they've got a really good story to tell. Here's an example:

> When I was younger, my parents had a green Datsun B210 with tan fake leather seats. We lived down south, so the interior of that car was always blazing. We'd get in the backseat and our legs would immediately stick to the "leather" and then the sweating would start and we'd be sliding all over. It was miserable. Add to that an annoying little brother and the result was frequent arguments in the back of that car. My mother had perfected a reach-around pointer finger technique that allowed her to wag, while driving, at my brother and

me as we continued to argue and misbehave. On one extraordinarily annoying day, I began to yell at my brother so he would know how insanely stupid I thought he was. I erupted, telling him at the top of my lungs, that he was *stupendous*, and immediately noticed my mother's pointer finger in action. The finger didn't complete the action, though, as my mother stopped short and I saw a smile erupt across her face in the rearview mirror. She said that was the nicest thing I'd ever said to my brother. She explained what the word meant, and its meaning is burned into my brain like a cattle branding. Even these many years later it still stings. But, as it turns out, my brother *is* stupendous; I just didn't know it then.

Step 3: Construct meaning socially.

Teachers, as coaches, should navigate students through their thinking and pull out important facets, helping them to construct, at least at a base level, a workable definition of new words. Create definitions, at least partially, from analyzing context, root word knowledge, and prefixes or suffixes. Workable definitions can also come from their receptive vocabulary—words that they've integrated into their oral language but have not yet transitioned to their expressive vocabulary where they know the word well enough to write it or use it to create some demonstration of learning. This social construction of meaning builds on prior knowledge bases. Effective teachers help students to build on a foundation of pieces that students already own. Social construction of meaning can also be engaged using virtual tools such as Today's Meet or Padlet, where students might virtually contribute text, images, and video to build meaning in expressive ways. This would be a boon to engagement, offering students opportunities to share perspectives, which could in turn act as scaffolding for students who need it.

Step 4: Allow students to identify words that they want to learn.

New vocabulary acquisition should be contextual and authentic. In addition to words that the teacher thinks are important or that the teacher has identified as potential roadblocks in a text, solicit student-generated words for vocabulary lists. These words might not be ones a teacher might intend, but if students feel the need to go deeper with words they don't know or understand fully, they should be allowed to do so. This enriches their experiences with words and gives them a sense of being valued and invited to learn what is meaningful for them. It would be especially important for students in younger grade levels to be able to say that they had trouble understanding this word or that word, and to have those words added to their word study or word work.

Step 5: Play games with words.

Playing games with words allows students a trial and error space, a sandbox, to try out the words or practice fluency or build knowledge through activities that aren't the traditional rote. This ultimately helps students retain the new words they are learning.

One of the fun things my oldest daughter and I do in the car or on walks around the neighborhood is to amuse ourselves with words that have multiple meanings. I might see a squirrel and I'll ask her to define the word "squirrel" in her own words. Then I'll tell her that it also has a different meaning and talk about being distracted. We'll have conversations about "squirreling" on someone in a conversation or even a squirrel getting distracted from its own mission to bury acorns and climbing a nearby tree.

Step 6: Engage in constant formative assessment.

Constant formative assessment is necessary. Knowing whether or not students are "getting it" is an obligation in every classroom. In the

"What You Can Do Tomorrow" section, I wrote about listening for students to use the new words orally and observing students using the new words in writing. Extend these practices throughout the school year. Teachers should be on a constant quest to determine whether or not students are understanding and applying new learning. This certainly could happen on a unit test, but effective teachers are going to be looking for evidence of understanding and application so that potential opportunities for improvement don't have to wait a week or two before a more formal assessment occurs.

Step 7: Read. Read. Read.

Independent reading at an instructional reading level is essential to developing strong, vocabulary-savvy readers. Although reading grade-level texts, such as with guided reading, is clearly necessary, positive interactions with a broad range of texts creates flexible, fluent readers and thinkers. Still, students need to be reading at instructional reading levels as much as possible to access more text and thus more words. Lots and lots of reading at a student's instructional level is the best way to develop good readers and build high-level vocabulary toolboxes. You do not tell an athlete how awesome running is and then expect him or her to win the race without practice. The athlete has to run often and far to be a better runner. Analysis of running technique is valuable, but even learning from this sort of focused assessment does not negate the necessity to run. Reading works the same way.

OVERCOMING PUSHBACK

TWWADI: This is "The Way We've Always Done It." Just because a practice is traditional, or habituated, or widespread doesn't mean it's a good one. We can't continue to perpetuate ineffective instructional practices. This is a challenge, a provocation to do what's best for students rather than what's easy for adults. Continuing to engage in vocabulary-building practices that have been proven not to work is like ignoring the fact that even though a lighter will create a fire more efficiently and faster, you're happy rubbing two sticks together, regardless of how long it takes to get a spark, if you get a spark at all. Our students can't wait for the fire to be built. Ditch the tradition and start a bonfire.

The curriculum we purchased already includes vocabulary instruction. Most of them do. However, as I've said, the vendor does not know your population of students as you do, nor does that vendor necessarily understand all the facets of effective vocabulary instruction. You, on the other hand, know your students and, after having read to this point in this chapter, you should have a pretty good handle on how you can enhance vocabulary instruction in your classroom. Look at the vocabulary processes in your vendor product. Assume that they are basic, like cheese pizza. What can you add to it to enhance the flavor and the pizza experience? How much more do you need to *pronounce, engage,* and *assess*?

THE HACK IN ACTION

Over the last couple of years, I've had the opportunity to do some teaching on Skype with classrooms around the country. In one of those virtual teaching situations, I worked with a group of fourth graders in an elementary school in Jacksonville, Florida. We were working on improving their writing practice and I was offering whole-class feedback on work that they had submitted to me via email.

While reading through their writing I noticed some global factors that would make useful mini-lessons. A couple of those global factors had to do with word choices and details in their writing. In the course of sharing this feedback with them, I offered a blanket statement about being "emphatic" writers.

One of the students immediately raised her hand and asked what "emphatic" meant. I stopped my mini-lesson to address this new vocabulary word. I asked if anyone in the classroom knew what "emphatic" meant. No hands went up. I asked them to think about words that sounded similar to the word "emphatic." One student offered "static," but another offered "emphasis." I reminded the students that while "static" might be a rhyming word, the word "emphasis" was in the same word family.

I asked the students if anyone knew what the word "emphasis" meant. Several hands went up. Of those students with their hands up, I asked one to read a selection from his writing for the class, but to read with "emphasis." The student read with intense expression, punctuating several of the words while he read.

I asked the class again how many students knew what emphasis meant. More hands went up. I asked students who could tell me a definition of the word. I called on several students to explain. Their answers included:

"Reading something loud."

"I think it means that something is important."

"Does it mean that something is special and we need to pay attention to it?"

I told them that all were right. I explained that "emphasis" and "emphatic" were in the same word family and had similar meanings. So, now that they knew what "emphasis" meant, I asked them what they thought I might mean by being "emphatic writers." Here's what they came up with:

"Maybe we should make sure we're writing about something important."

"Sometimes we should read what we write and see if it makes sense."

"Is this about the details you were talking about? Do we need good details?"

"I can emphasize something important by adding more details, right?"

We had a quick discussion of the word "emphasize" being part of the "emphasis" word family. One student looked the word up on an online dictionary on one of the class iPads. When he read the definition out loud, it included something along the lines of "expressing ideas forcefully and clearly." We discussed which of the meanings made the most sense to the group and they emphatically chose their own definitions.

This entire scenario took only a few minutes and we were able to get back to our mini-lesson. After I was done with the virtual session, the teacher added "emphatic" to the list of words they were working on. She noticed that several students began using it immediately when they spoke, and some even used it in their writing in subsequent weeks. Note that this scenario had a natural and authentic flow to it rather than being a stand-alone, and perhaps forced, word lesson. It represents an opportunity to engage in vocabulary instruction at the moment that vocabulary instruction is needed. Note that I *pronounced* the word, I *engaged* with a couple of quick activities to determine its meaning, and I did a quick formative *assessment* before I went back into the mini-lesson. The classroom teacher followed up with continued usage of the word and subsequent observations of how it was being used in speaking and in writing.

I wholeheartedly believe that a process-oriented approach to vocabulary instruction is the key to maximum student learning and performance. Over the last few years, it's taken some convincing to get teachers to understand that the way we've always done it won't work for contemporary students. Vocabulary instruction has to be relevant and authentic: It needs to be just in time versus just in case.

EMBRACE THE NOVEL

Debunk the 70/30 delusion

*I did then what I knew how to do. Now
that I know better, I do better.*
—MAYA ANGELOU, POET

THE PROBLEM: MISGUIDED DIRECTIVES
TO ELIMINATE LITERATURE

SINCE THE COMMON Core Standards were introduced, there has
been much discussion in the media about the shift to informational
text. In some cases, teachers were told to stop teaching literature in favor
of informational texts that are intended to build background knowledge.

The rationale behind this mass pivot toward informational text centers
on an innocuous table on page 5 of the Common Core State Standards
for English Language Arts. The problem lies in its misinterpretation.
The table and its explanatory information describe the framework of the
2009 National Assessment of Educational Progress (NAEP exam). They
do not suggest a teacher is responsible to eliminate literary texts.

Let's dissect page 5.

The table at the top of the page represents the distribution of literary and informational texts in grades 4, 8, and 12 on the NAEP exam. Those distributions are 50/50, 45/55, and 30/70 for the respective grade levels.

The first sentence after the chart states, "The Standards aim to align instruction with this framework." The rest of the first paragraph details the types of informational text and literary nonfiction that should balance with fiction in student reading. There's also a sentence that states, "a great deal of informational reading in grades 6-12 must take place in other classes." That's other classes, apart from the ELA class.

Surface-skimming teachers and administrators have created and supported some commonly held misconceptions that I see in multiple districts around the country. These misconceptions include:

- 70 percent of all text in every grade level must be informational.

- If having 70 percent informational text is an improvement, then we can do even better by going for 100 percent informational text and removing literary texts altogether.

- 70 percent of all text should be literary.

- ELA teachers are solely responsible for this shift.

THE HACK: EMBRACE THE NOVEL AND TEACH LITERATURE

I'm not sure why such wild interpretations gained credence, but this is where the hack comes into play. Don't ditch literary texts altogether; instead, spread responsibility for balanced reading among all teachers in the school.

Also of note is the first footnote on page 5 of the CCSS for English Language Arts, which states that for 12th grade, "70 percent of student reading across the grade should be informational." The important words here, "across the grade," indicate that this percentage of informational text is not the sole responsibility of the ELA teacher.

Understand what's really supposed to be going on:

- Every teacher's identity should be shifting to that of a supporter of reading, particularly with regard to domain-specific informational texts that help build background knowledge across all subjects.

- Including 70 percent informational text is intended for 12th grade.

- That 70 percent informational text should be integrated across multiple content areas, not just ELA.

> **Literary fiction engages students, and that engagement hooks kids into a lifelong love of reading.**

- ELA teachers should *not* be eliminating literary texts from the curriculum. The Common Core does not support this.

- ELA teachers should be enhancing comprehension of literary texts with supporting informational texts. (This is not a specific piece of evidence from page 5; it's just a general comment based on my knowledge of the standards and the PARCC content frameworks.)

Bottom line: Every teacher in every school is responsible for the reading detailed on page 5, but with the understanding that the percentages are not a specific set of instructional rules. They are only a framework for instructional ideas based on the NAEP assessment.

Compartmentalizing who learns what where is not necessarily a benefit to overall learning. We should be looking to integrate and overlap and connect. Read the documents that direct our instructional decisions closely.

WHAT **YOU** CAN DO TOMORROW

- **Teach informational texts effectively.** The explicit teaching of informational and background-building texts goes far beyond just providing them for students. Active reading across all subject areas is necessary for this hack to work. That means that we must choose texts with a degree of complexity that is appropriate for the grade level and readiness of the students. Informational text is often more difficult to comprehend than literary text because of the number of unknown and perhaps domain-specific words. Guided reading and conversations about evidence and conclusion are essential here, as is assessing both the receptive and expressive capabilities of the students.

- **Let students read.** Independent reading is the single most essential thing that a child should be doing. Teachers across all content areas and grade levels should devote as much time as possible to this endeavor. If you want higher performing students, students with absolute readiness for the next grade's challenges, and students who are ready for the world they will graduate into, then give them the gift of reading time. As a bonus perk, proficient readers score higher on standardized tests, though I'm not advocating for that as a primary reason to read more.

- **Read beyond school too.** They should be reading outside of school too, but I'm a realist when it comes to how much actually gets done at home. My children virtually live with Fountas and Pinnell and we can't make it happen every single night, but we do try to make it an integral part of our evening routine. Know that students will be far more likely to read on their own time if they are able to make their own choices of books that interest them. Teach them to "sneak read," to open their books whenever they can sneak a few minutes of reading into their days—while waiting for the school bus, before the basketball game begins, or waiting for a show to start.

A BLUEPRINT FOR FULL IMPLEMENTATION

Step 1: Provide ongoing professional development on content-area literacy.

Look to your science and social studies teachers for tricks and tips—they've been using informational texts for decades. Which of their processes for analyzing informational texts would apply across other content areas? Get the science and social studies teachers to share some of their teaching practices in faculty meetings.

Schools often benefit from having a literacy coach on site. This is a person who can provide ongoing feedback about balanced literacy, content literacy, the connections between reading and writing, and curriculum help to integrate literacy seamlessly into any content area. If having a literacy coach is outside of your school's budget, consider a buddy/team system approach to literacy, where every member of your staff is a contributor of literacy ideas. Dedicate a faculty meeting or two at the beginning of a school year just to literacy so you can develop and leverage the professional talent in your organization to create an expansive literacy-focused culture.

Step 2: Talk to your administrators and colleagues.

Make sure you understand exactly what page 5 of the Common Core English Language Arts document advocates, describes, and emphasizes. Discuss this as a learning team and draw informed conclusions about how to balance informational and literary text.

Step 3: Get everybody in the boat.

Make sure that every person in your learning organization knows the shared responsibility for engaging with texts. If you're a teacher, realize that it is your responsibility to enhance literacy skills in your class. This might look different from one class to another, but keep in mind that literacy skills take many forms and that listening and speaking are equally important.

Step 4: Assess the texts you use.

This is a good opportunity to look at text complexity in general across your programs and grade levels. Look to Appendix A in the Common Core to find information about text complexity so you understand what it is that makes a text complex. It's not just a lexile level. Teachers need to understand qualitative aspects of a text as well as reader and task considerations. For more information on text complexity, go to *LiveBinders.com* and search for "Text Complexity Resources." Look for my username: MikeFisher821 to make sure you have the right binder. There are tons of tools in that binder to help you make decisions around text complexity.

Step 5: Let Dorothy return to Oz:

If you removed the literary fiction from your ELA class, bring it back. Literary fiction engages students, and that engagement hooks kids into a lifelong love of reading. Forcing them to read nothing but informational text (particularly if it is all chosen by the teacher) builds more roadblocks to reading than background knowledge. Speaking of teacher choice: Don't necessarily keep teaching the same novels you've always taught just for the sake of their purported cultural importance or your comfort. Think about the thematic elements in those novels you enjoy teaching. Perhaps some recent novels that share those themes would be worth exploring and more engaging. You might pair a new novel to a more traditional one for the sake of analysis, comparison, and evaluation. Note that the PARCC Model Frameworks for the structure of a unit plan in English language arts suggests that each anchor text in a unit (whether it's literary or informational) has at least some informational text support. This support could be short articles, news items, web resources, infographics, or anything else that enhances a student's understanding of ideas and themes in a primary text.

Step 6: Look for opportunities to be a literacy ecosystem.

Every living thing has a niche in an ecosystem. Likewise, every person in your learning organization needs to both define and participate in a niche, whatever it might be. Where are your overlaps? Where are there opportunities beyond the English language arts class to develop literacy in any form: reading, writing, listening, or speaking? All of these elements integrate when everyone is participating. If all parts of the system do their individual jobs, the system will become self-sustaining.

OVERCOMING PUSHBACK

I have enough to do. Literacy is not my responsibility. Invite these teachers to consider what literacy already exists in their classrooms. Music is a language, art involves analysis and interpretation, and physical education is comprised of skills developed through listening, speaking, and action. Even if it's subtle, literacy opportunities exist everywhere. Literacy is not added to content area work; good literacy practice supports better learning in the content areas.

We'll have to redo all of our lessons and units. If you find that your proportion of literary to informational texts is out of balance, it is not necessary to redo the lessons and units. Adjustments would be more along the lines of making sure that you create balance between text types and ensure that texts support each other. There's an extension here, too, involving multimedia. Units and lessons should be opportunities for engaging with multiple types of media, including traditional print, pictures, videos, infographics, and other texts. The real world operates in multimedia and we're not doing our students any favors by focusing on just one medium.

If your curriculum centers on a particular resource, such as a certain novel, then revise the units and lessons so they may be used with any text or resource. Instead of focusing on that one text, represent standards and skill sets, offer opportunities for engagement and creativity, and include assessments. Teachers should be able to articulate the skills that they are teaching, not just that they are teaching *To Kill a Mockingbird* or *Fahrenheit 451*.

THE HACK IN ACTION

A year or so ago, comedian Louis C. K. started a firestorm on Twitter by tweeting about the Common Core assessments his kids were taking. Many shared his frustrations about testing and trusting teachers. Much of what he said was spot on, particularly his assertion that "everything important is worth doing carefully." I think about his words when I talk to teachers about the Common Core Standards and how to separate the standards from the flurry of minutiae around them.

When we're not careful or purposeful, errors happen. In the case of implementing the Common Core, mistakes and misinterpretations occur when we act too swiftly on misinformation, and we may not even understand what it is that we lose. Misunderstanding what the

Common Core asks for in terms of informational texts has resulted in careless mistakes.

I saw instances of misapplication in multiple schools around the United States, the most egregious of which was a school district in the Midwest that chose to remove much of the literature from grades 9-12. When I arrived to help with their curricular upgrades, the teachers explained how upset they were with what their district administration had mandated in the redesign.

They had already integrated many more informational texts into their teaching, and some problems were emerging. They had chosen mostly short texts—current event articles, historical documents, databases, biographical excerpts, etc. They intentionally had looked for texts that they thought would be timely and interesting for the students, but reported that some students were struggling with the vocabulary in these selections. These teachers also noted that in general, the students were interested and somewhat engaged in the texts.

The bigger problem was what that engagement really meant. Teachers told me that the students would read and answer the associated questions, but they had lost the rich conversations that they previously had with the literary texts. This was extraordinarily significant and extremely troubling to me. What these teachers were describing as engagement was really just being on task. Students did what they were told and the learning, if any, was "one and done." Sounds kind of like an office environment doesn't it? Do what you're supposed to do and clock out at the end of the period. These teachers weren't describing a school, they were describing a factory.

During our morning break, I invited the assistant superintendent for curriculum and instruction and the high school principal to join me for an hour with the teachers. For the sake of group understanding and consistency, I shared the page 5 document about the

NAEP exam results, pointing out the footnote, and I also shared with them some specific reading standards for their consideration.

We explored grade level standards side by side, particularly those in the strand designation for the integration of knowledge and ideas (Reading Standards 7-9) in both literary and informational texts. I pointed out that there are specific authors and titles exemplified in the grade-specific standards in high school and shared with them Appendix B, which includes text exemplars for each grade level or grade band. This appendix provides examples of text that run the gamut of literary and informational texts. The main point I was trying to make is that eliminating literary texts is not what the Common Core calls for. It simply demands a better balance between the two text types and some consideration for using more informational texts across classes in the grade level so the responsibility for text and text interactions is shared.

I reminded the group that there are two separate sets of standards for reading, a set for literature and a set for informational text. If the Common Core advocates reading only non-fiction, then why include two sets of standards?

The group understood what I was saying and that's when the real curriculum upgrades could begin. I invited them to check out the PARCC (Partnership for the Assessment of Readiness for College and Careers) Content Frameworks for English Language Arts. While this was not a state that was using the PARCC assessments, I made an executive decision to share the framework as an example of how a unit plan could be organized. Broadly, this organization includes an anchor text (either literary or informational), several short supporting texts, a research opportunity, and writing. The organization of the framework is aligned to the Common Core Standards and isn't dependent on a singular resource. Our conversation continued around essential skills and brainstorming potential traditional and contemporary literary texts and additional texts we might use to support thematic elements or claims in the texts.

Before we wrapped up our time together, I asked the teachers to think about inviting rich conversation and real engagement back into their practice. There was a collective sigh of relief. If we reduce or eliminate the literary texts, then we reduce or eliminate passionate engagement with reading.

We definitely don't want to do that.

In short, we need to analyze the breadth of informational text used across a grade level. The Common Core Standards ask that students have experiences with both types of text, but make it clear that it's not necessarily the English language arts teachers' responsibility. We should be asking where literacy works into every class in a school.

HACK 6

PRIORITIZE

Make the standards work for you

It is not a daily increase. It is a daily decrease.
Hack away at the inessentials.
—Bruce Lee, Martial Artist

THE PROBLEM: STANDARDS ALIGNMENT IS OVERWHELMING

UNFORTUNATELY, THE BREADTH of the Common Core is overwhelming. This is the root of many Common Core implementation problems. Many teachers feel like they are barely scratching the surface of learning due to following prescribed curriculum with fidelity or teaching to the new Common Core tests. This leaves many teachers asking how they can make sound instructional decisions and still align to the standards.

THE HACK: PRIORITIZE THE STANDARDS

To truly make a difference in student learning, teachers need to understand that some of the standards have priority over others. Common Core purists might argue that each standard is necessary

> **Your job isn't to teach *to* a test but to teach *for* success on any assessment.**

and important; the reality is that narrow bands of standards are being assessed and some standards have a high degree of overlap.

When working with curriculum design in any form, the best approach is one step at a time. Often, educators get bogged down with the big picture, particularly when administrators have an "I need this done yesterday" mindset. Journeys are taken in steps, though: Reach goals by setting manageable and attainable targets.

Prioritizing the standards deepens learning, strengthens curriculum design efforts, and creates better learning experiences for students. Once teachers determine their priorities, they align curriculum accordingly.

WHAT YOU CAN DO TOMORROW

- **Look at tomorrow's assessments, or whichever ones are coming up soon.** Are the standards representative of those that are repeated across the instructional year? Do they address something peripheral or essential? Don't be afraid to delete assessment elements that are not related to critical or priority standards, unless the standards associated with those elements are essential for foundational knowledge or are building lifelong skills.

- **Change the preposition.** Your job isn't to teach *to* a test but to teach *for* success on any assessment. Teaching is both an art and a science, meaning that teachers are like scientist-artists. They must know the theoretical basis for what they do, but also create engaging opportunities for students to learn well beyond the curricular goals. Working above a standard is a good thing. It means that students will be prepared for any test at any time.

• **Think in bundles.** Know what standards go together both thematically and conceptually. In the math standards, conceptual groupings are built in. In the ELA standards, teachers must have an awareness of analogues and relationships. For instance, when you ask students to find evidence in a text, the activity engages reading standards one through three. These standards, in an expressive capacity, are related to writing standards one and two, where students write using evidence from a text. We will also find natural relationships to speaking and listening standards when we consider the extent of what a student might learn and demonstrate around textual evidence. Considering bundled standards instead of individual standards allows the teacher to teach with more precision and the learner to learn more deeply.

A BLUEPRINT FOR FULL IMPLEMENTATION

Step 1: Identify what will be assessed.

Across the country, state education departments publish testing guides well before state assessments occur. These guides tell educators specifically which standards a test will assess, though they don't say how often a particular standard will be represented. In the New York testing guide, for example, middle grades ELA assessments will focus up to 65 percent of the multiple choice questions on the first three standards for literature and informational text. Out of 42 standards, that's a focus on just six. While subsequent sections of the assessment address additional standards, the test still assesses a very narrow band of standards, and not the entire breadth of the Common Core. Consider it this way:

If you are in a PARCC (Partnership for the Assessment of Readiness in College and Careers) state or an SBAC (Smarter Balanced Assessment Consortium) state, you could look to the PARCC Model Frameworks or the Smarter Balanced Assessment Blueprint for information to help you focus attention on standards that represent priorities. For example, in math, concentrate on fluency, concept building, and connections to other standards. If you don't know about testing guides or assessment overviews for your state, ask your administrator or search your state's education website with key terms such as: *testing manual, testing guide, assessment guide, assessment overview, test or assessment framework,* etc.

Step 2: Discern which outcomes have leverage in other classes.

Determine standards priorities by considering leverage and which standards have a high degree of overlap in other classes and content areas. For instance, if students are learning about ratios in math, there is a strong possibility that they will also be learning about them in health, physical education, sciences, or career and tech ed. classes. Those teachers who teach about ratios should collaborate about teaching methods and holding students accountable for their learning. This would be an excellent time to have a conversation about an integrated project or some type of authentic performance-based problem.

Step 3: Identify lifelong skills.

Any concept or idea students learn that will serve them into the future, such as understanding text structures or knowing multiplication tables, is considered a lifelong skill. Fluency in sight words and math facts should have a level of automaticity for students so that they have access to more challenging problems and texts. If they don't understand the basics, they are going to struggle with anything more complex. Gaps occur in important lifelong skills when teachers cover curriculum superficially because of time or administrative constraints and students don't really get the foundational elements of a content area. Missing that foundation is detrimental to subsequent learning, leading to ever-widening gaps in proficiency, as students get older. Teachers must make sure they understand how standards inform lifelong skills, but they must also understand how their professional knowledge as effective educators allows them to determine these skills.

Step 4: Evaluate student readiness.

An extension to lifelong skills, or perhaps as a subset of it, is student readiness. It is imperative that students are prepared to move to the next level of sophistication. They cannot be dragged into learning for which they are not yet ready. Pushing students before they have the capacity to learn also forms gaps over time and their frustration creates lifelong anti-learners who aren't willing to try. We certainly don't want that.

Step 5: Know what teacher evaluation entails.

All of the states with new teacher evaluations are using either newly approved state level teaching standards or existing teacher effectiveness rubrics, such as Charlotte Danielson's Domains of Professional Practice. If you're overwhelmed by the language of the new teacher effectiveness standards or the rubrics associated with teacher effectiveness, look back to Hack 1 on the instructional shifts, college and career readiness capacities, and mathematical practices. Making sure that these are aggressively represented in your curriculum and your everyday practice will make any observation a piece of cake.

Step 6: Ensure that your curriculum frequently presents priority standards.

Dig into your curriculum to find redundancy and overlap with your priority standards. Priority standards need not be engaged the same way in every class, but they should emerge with regularity as you design and enhance curricular units over the course of the year.

Step 7: Reorganize and re-imagine your curriculum to reflect priorities.

Some aspects of Common Core skills are assessment anchors on Core assessments around the country, such as analytical reading, foundational math concepts, and scaffolds for sophisticated demonstrations of learning. These skills should be represented with regularity in your curriculum.

Note: The tips in this Blueprint for understanding priorities are a mash-up of several people's work: Fenwick English, Heidi Hayes-Jacobs, Janet Hale, Larry Ainsworth, and Susan Udelhoffen. If you're looking to develop a more structured system around the prioritization of standards, Common Core or otherwise, look for publications by these fine folks.

OVERCOMING PUSHBACK

We already use a vendor product or have curriculum maps. Then it's time for a friendly appraisal. How clear is your documented curriculum? How contemporary is it? How often does it address the identified priorities? Does it align instruction and assessment in both skill level and cognition? These are among the important questions to ask and topics to brainstorm regarding a purchased curriculum or one that hasn't been upgraded in years, particularly since the onset of the Common Core. Gather a team and start digging in, keeping anything that will truly benefit student learning or that aligns to the priority standards. Cut the rest, especially if you are struggling to fit everything in, which often happens with vendor products.

We already revised our assessments to align with the state tests. One of the traps that teachers are falling into when implementing the Common Core Standards is in "aligning" their benchmark or quarterly assessments to new standards but not really changing their instruction all that much. This is probably the number one thing that teachers tell me when I come in to work with them on curriculum. I've heard all of the excuses and I've seen numerous solutions. Many of those solutions come down to teachers asking themselves two questions: 1) Does my professional practice truly represent what is in the best interest of my students, and 2) Am I trying to hang on to the way I've always done it? Make sure that your priorities are pervasive in the system. Whatever conversations you had about standards priorities for the sake of assessment revisions, invite those conversations about instructional practice revisions too.

THE HACK IN ACTION

Due to poor performance on grades 3-8 English language arts assessments aligned to the Common Core, several districts across a region in central North Carolina got their kindergarten through eighth grade English language arts teachers together to determine the priority skills that should be taught during each quarter of the school year. These districts had different documented curricula and were not attempting to reach consensus on adopting one curriculum over another; rather, they were meeting to define skills and associated standards, leaving instructional resources and even assessments up to the individual districts.

> **Find the priorities, look for overlaps, and work smarter, not harder.**

At the initial meeting, grade-level teachers met for 3-4 hours to share their curriculum documents. Teachers later met as individual districts to document the skills they taught in the first quarter. They coded these skills as primary skills, mastery skills, and supporting skills, which were important but subordinate to the primary skills.

Once teachers in each district had determined their lists of first-quarter skills, they shared them with the other grade-level teachers. The initial combined list was long and represented many of the Common Core Standards. In order to pare the list down to a manageable level, the teachers wrote each of the standards that they identified as "essential" or "priority" on individual sticky notes and put them on tables around the room. Each teacher went around to the individual sticky notes and recorded a "✓," an "X," or a "?" on each note, with "?" meaning that they weren't sure if it was a priority or not.

Teams included the standards that had the most "✓s" on the skills map that they eventually created. They aligned each of these skills to a specific Common Core Standard and the teachers made sure that all skills from the standard were represented on the map. Once they separated the document by strands for reading (literary and informational text), writing, speaking and listening, language, and foundations, everything was typed up to share amongst the districts. They later revised to include some additional skills they had discussed and agreed upon.

They repeated this process for each of the other quarters. When teachers met for subsequent meetings, they added the assessments that their schools were using to the map for the sake of transparency for all schools involved.

Because of the conversations involved in creating this priority skills/standards map, teachers developed a deeper understanding of the standards. They used the map to upgrade their documented curriculum for consistency across the region and better alignment to the Common Core.

An immediate effect emerged in the form of better scores on local benchmark and quarterly assessments. Since this is an ongoing project, we do not yet have the current year's state assessment results, but the teachers are more confident about what they are doing and have a better understanding of what the Common Core demands. They also feel like they have better professional control of their curriculum, as they are now in the habit of discussing their curriculum, its alignment to the standards, how to collaborate to do better work, and how to improve their individual professional practices.

Note that this process for standards prioritization is a foundational element in mapping the curriculum and has been written about by Heidi Hayes Jacobs, Larry Ainsworth, Janet Hale, Grant Wiggins, and Jay McTighe.

Finding the priorities that exist in the standards, based on the blueprint and your knowledge of your students, is an important step in aligning to the Common Core Standards. It's also an opportunity to remove some of the overwhelming feelings that you may be having when considering the breadth of the standards. Find the priorities, look for overlaps, and work smarter, not harder.

VIGOR VERSUS RIGOR

Meet the challenge without becoming paralyzed

*More options, even good ones, can freeze us
and make us retreat to the default plan.*
—CHIP HEATH, AUTHOR

THE PROBLEM: IT'S NOT AS RIGOROUS AS YOU THINK

RIGOR HAS BEEN one of the buzziest educational words since the advent of the Common Core. Vendors have honed in on rigor as a selling point, highlighting the term to market their wares. The bigger the company, the more intense the rigor, or at least that's what they'd have you believe. There's big money in being the most rigorous version of Common Core aligned materials available. The real problem is these products aren't necessarily as rigorous as they think they are.

There's a big difference between more work and better work. Vendors, who don't know your population of kids personally, should never be the ones directing traffic in your classroom. Perhaps it would be beneficial to closely read the documents associated with your vendor product.

Does it rely heavily on a particular strategy or type of formative assessment, such as close reading each page of a story or using exit tickets at the end of every lesson? Does it include more practice with mathemat-

Vigor is the word you're really looking for.

ical problems or more comprehension questions than there were in previous iterations of the resource? Do its prescriptive steps negate the need for you to have a teaching degree to deliver the material? Are the materials geared toward a generalized audience of students?

That's not rigor. That's just more stuff with a side of distrust in your abilities. Common sense and Common Core aren't mutually exclusive.

THE HACK: GO DEEP WITH VIGOR INSTEAD

This is a one-letter hack. Change the first "r" in rigor to a "v." Vigor is the word you're really looking for. I know it's just semantics, but sometimes changing little things has a big impact. We're seeking opportunities for depth. We're seeking authentic growth with engagement. I don't think depth, authentic growth, or engagement will happen when we focus so intently on rigor, a word that connotes strictness, severity, and stiffness.

Vigor, conversely, connotes robustness, health, strength, and hardiness. It makes me think of dynamic and enthusiastic learning, of interactive and innovative learning environments, and of organic and authentic learning moments. All things I associate with depth. Vigor is a word that makes me think of the joy in learning—perhaps the joy *of* learning. I've written much over the years about engagement in the learning process. You can't have real learning if you don't have real engagement. Students need an emotional anchor. They need something to connect to that they aren't likely to forget. Vigorous learning experiences provide anchors for real learning.

This means that we need to consider how vigorous our curriculum is in light of the Common Core Standards. Skills are important, but equally so are imagination, creativity, and inquiry. They should never be separated.

WHAT **YOU** CAN DO TOMORROW

1. **Appraise your current week's curriculum.** Take out this week's plan and look for items that are invigorating and items that are the monotonous same-old, same-old. Replace anything boring with something more exciting. For instance, if math practice consists of a worksheet or an often-used strategy, switch it up with some manipulatives. Call out a number and have students use the manipulatives to create visual equations as quickly as possible. Use pennies, buttons, checkers, or anything you've got. Perhaps your students are drawing angles or shapes. What about a field trip around the school to take pictures of the angles or shapes you're studying? Come back to the classroom and organize the pictures. Use rulers and protractors to measure the images and compare what you collected. Perhaps students are taking a spelling or vocabulary test. Have them use the words to tell a story orally first, then ask them to write down as much of the story as they can remember, maybe using a digital tool like Storybird or Google Docs. Be sure to add visuals for maximum engagement.

2. **Share your intentions.** Let your colleagues or teammates know what you're thinking and look for opportunities to share vigorous practices. Talk regularly with your grade level or content area team about your engagement strategies for the coming

week. Share your plans and create opportunities to brainstorm about each other's work.

3. Practice engagement habits. Engagement habits will help you to work fun into your curriculum. Get into the habit of asking yourself two questions: 1) How often am I creating engaging opportunities for my students? and 2) In what ways am I creating engaging opportunities for my students? Easy and effective answers to these two questions involve offering choices to students. Those choices could include differentiated products, processes, media, technology tools, or even choices in assessments.

4. Ask the students. In the 21st century, student voice and input is essential to buy-in and real learning more than ever. Provide your students with opportunities to make decisions about how they will learn and demonstrate their learning. Note how those choices positively affect their learning and determine which types of choices help students to do their best work. Students need to know that their voices are being heard and valued. Students need to know that their opinions matter and that they have choices in the way that they learn something and the way that they will be assessed.

A BLUEPRINT FOR FULL IMPLEMENTATION

Step 1: Appraise your curriculum.

Systematically look at your yearlong curriculum. Start with the current unit and work your way forward. If you're reading this mid-year, it's fine to wait until the summer to revise the units you've already completed. Look for opportunities to inject joy, creativity, awe, technology, PBL, STEAM, engagement, and personalization. Vigor is like seasoning. Put it in every recipe! To beef up the zest and robustness of your curriculum, makes sure the verbs in your unit plans match the verbs in the standards. Adjust verbs in assessments so they match as well. Appraise your curriculum for thinking. Vigorous units, while being engaging, should also scaffold thinking. Certainly, students should be able to recognize and identify content pieces, but they need many opportunities to apply, evaluate, and create too. All levels of thinking should be in a vigorous curriculum.

Step 2: Create a culture of shared curriculum design.

Converse, collaborate, and come to consensus with all stakeholders. Sometimes you can discover meaningful ways to engage, teach, or assess by asking your colleagues and your students. Document these conversations in your curriculum units and remind everyone in the design process how valuable their input is. Share goals and objectives with students ahead of time and ask them about their vision for demonstrating how they might get there. Add their ideas to the plan or let them create a menu of options that would allow them some choice in activities and assessments.

Step 3: Make learning fun again.

Let's get back to what really matters in learning. Vigorous learning makes acquisition and application of knowledge so memorable that teachers can simultaneously engage enduring understandings and work above the curriculum, virtually guaranteeing that students will never forget what they've learned/participated in/created. Vigorous learning spans differentiations, includes everyone's unique contributions, and gives kids the voices they need. If they are participators (through action, design, conversation, etc.), then they are learners.

Let me say that again: *If the kids are participators, they are learners.* Purposeful design and purposeful practice prompt so many implications for learning and making that learning stick.

Step 4: Introduce PBL and STEM/STEAM.

In problem based learning (PBL), students seek to solve an authentic problem using research skills and critical thinking while building content knowledge. STEM and STEAM have to do with engineering tasks, creating a product using related science, technology, math, and arts skills.

> **Learning shouldn't be the soupe du jour; it should be a buffet.**

In some schools, the emphasis is on the science or the technology or the mathematics, but in my experience, engineering the product should be the focal point, with the other content areas orbiting it. Having PBL or STEM/STEAM projects in your curriculum open up multiple options for students to research and study authentic projects and issues, building opportunities for engagement and deep learning. Real engagement is where joy and awe live in the curriculum.

OVERCOMING PUSHBACK

We don't have time for fun. There's a scene in the movie *Hocus Pocus* when the witches in the story come across a school in Salem, Massachusetts. The other witches ask what this building is and Bette Midler's character, Winifred, takes a look at the drab exterior, the peeling paint, the wrought iron and pointy fence, and determines that it is a prison for children. When teachers tell me that they don't have time for fun or joy or awe or depth, this is what I think of. If teachers aren't providing experiences their students will remember, keeping everything "the way we've always done it," school certainly does sound like prison to me—imagine how the kids feel. What teachers are really saying when they say they don't have time for fun is that they don't have time for learning. It's never a surprise to me when baffled teachers tell me that they covered their curriculum and they did loads of test prep, but the kids still didn't perform. Why should they? Teachers didn't give them incentives to learn; they only provided students with opportunities to receive knowledge the way they receive candy from a Pez dispenser. That's not teaching or learning, and there's nothing in that method that makes the learning stick. If you really care about learning and performance, then you have to care about fun and engagement. They go hand-in-hand, like Forrest Gump and Jenny or peas and carrots.

The administrator wants vigor but also wants me to use a vendor product with a high degree of fidelity. As with other similar issues, the answer is that the team needs to talk. Conversation, collaboration, and consensus are really important here. You must talk about what's worth keeping and what needs to be deleted from your vendor products. If we want vigorous instruction and engagement, fun, and joy, then we have to think of our specific population of kids as a lens through which we look at the curriculum. We can't apply a generalized curriculum to a specific group of children in the same way we can't give aspirin to every malady and have it work. Curriculum needs to be targeted and focused like a laser for each specific population of students. If you must adhere to a vendor product, then you must evaluate its many facets. Use only the components and resources that benefit your students—chuck everything else. Then find ways to inject your class with joy and authenticity.

Our population of students is working nowhere near grade level, so how can I do more vigorous work with them? Vigor isn't necessarily in what is on grade level; rather, it is in what challenges the individual student. This means that teachers have to pay attention to their students' interests, their abilities, and their performances.

Teachers must analyze whether faulty performance is due to an interest issue or a learning issue. If it's lack of interest, then talk to the student and see if there is some alternate way for the student to demonstrate proficiency. If it's a gap in learning, scaffold instruction so that the student has a more manageable way to attain the goal. Offer more choices in the ways students learn and the ways they can demonstrate their learning. Learning shouldn't be the soupe du jour; it should be a buffet. Choices matter here, and the more choices a student has in learning and in assessment, the more accurately you can determine whether that student actually gets it. Students who have choices and are engaged will likely level up faster and attain grade-level expectations if they are supported appropriately.

THE HACK IN ACTION

In a city middle school in downtown Manhattan, teachers were frustrated with students' performance on the New York State Common Core Assessments. During professional development, teachers discussed how the scores were a "checkup," like taking a person's pulse at one moment in time, and they weren't meant to diagnose students' learning needs. However, the test scores had been low for two years in a row and they agreed that they needed to improve their approach.

This school had been using curriculum materials supplied to New York State by vendors who had won state contracts. There was a vendor for English language arts and a separate vendor for mathematics. Their administrator had tasked teachers with following the materials with fidelity, but clearly that level of adherence to the program was not getting them the results they wanted. While they didn't want to put all of their eggs in the state test basket, they were concerned that students were also underperforming on their benchmark assessments throughout the year despite the fact that teachers were steadfastly staying on track with their vendor-supplied curriculum.

I worked with these teachers to appraise their curriculum for contemporary practices. The teachers discovered that the vendor product was generalized for a large population. It didn't address what they believed were necessities, primarily regarding technology, choices in the learning process, and varied methods for formative and summative assessments.

We decided it would be beneficial to brainstorm opportunities to replace the generalized practices and assessments of the vendor products with more contemporary methods that truly represented their specific student population.

In particular, they looked at the products' assessments and instructional methodologies with an eye to integrating lively and contemporary revisions. They brainstormed ways to inject choice, fun, and authenticity into their instructional practices and brainstormed alternatives to the suggested assessments.

They also looked for opportunities for overlap in their professional practices and places to integrate content areas such as science and social studies into the language arts classes. They looked specifically at individual lesson plans and sought to replace rote activities with opportunities to explore and discover rather than "sit and get."

This school had begun mapping its curriculum even before the Common Core Standards had come into play. Teachers used existing curriculum mapping software to document the changes to the vendor's curriculum so that content area and grade-level decisions were visible to the whole organization.

Documenting their curriculum also conveniently pinpointed future professional development opportunities to address gaps and overlaps in the standards and to discuss their practical application. As of this publication, the school has yet to receive its current year's test scores, but the teachers feel confident that performance improved significantly because students were more engaged and had a more cerebral experience than in previous years. Students also performed better on benchmark assessments than they had since implementation of the Common Core Standards.

Many of the teachers commented on their improved morale when they heard students "oohing and aahing" over instructional activities that they had updated based on their collaborative conversations. After many years of feeling beaten down, they were finally starting to feel like they were making a difference again. There's no better feeling in the world for an educator.

Vigor doesn't mean heaping on more work. It means finding ways to engage students in opportunities for deep, rich learning. "The way we've always done it" won't work anymore, and neither will putting a fresh coat of paint on a traditional practice. We have to re-imagine contemporary teaching and learning, integrating vigor into instruction.

UPGRADE THE VERB

Take sophistication to a whole new level

People are always looking for the single magic bullet that will totally change everything. There is no single magic bullet.
—Temple Grandin, Author

THE PROBLEM: IT'S NOT THE STANDARDS THAT ARE PROBLEMATIC

THE WORK OF Wiggins and McTighe, Marzano, Jensen, Calkins, Fountas and Pinnell, Heidi Hayes Jacobs, Marie Clay, Karin Hess, Daniel Pink, and numerous others points to the fact that, while learning is expansive and difficult to compartmentalize, it is still possible to define learning progressions. We can trace progress as students move from beginning to emergent, gradually leading to fluent and sophisticated. Levels of progress are evident in all content areas, not just basic literacy and early numeracy. We must lay the foundation and then we build, build, build.

Regardless of which set of standards we use, and it's no secret that I think the Common Core Standards are in decent shape, problems get generated when people focus on trivialities associated with the standards. The educational buffoonery that goes on is the real problem. Common Core Standards aren't perfect, but they represent a good opportunity for us to analyze what we value as educators. Regardless of the nitpickery going on in Common Core states, I am baffled by the number of smart people who continue to direct their anger and energy at the wrong target. If we don't use these Common Core Standards, then what fixed points can we use to qualify consistency across the system? Previous standards? A return to the rote? Without a center point, the only option is to adopt "anything goes" as a model. Our students deserve more; we must begin to agree on basics and stop bickering over trivia.

Standards-based education has been around for a while. More than forty years, in fact. Our current Common Core Standards have evolved from a mid-70s shift toward providing a barometer for what all students should know and be able to do. We still need documentation of learning expectations across a student's journey through school. While the current standards are still delineated by individual years, I envision a time when we delineate by banded years, so that learners aren't limited by time but by learning. (This is potentially a future *Hack Learning* book!) In the meantime, we must learn to work within our current situation.

THE HACK: UPGRADE THE VERB AND ENHANCE THE STANDARDS

In the last forty years, educational research has exploded, leading us to examine the set points in our field. In much the same way that scientific research has led us to understand set points for cholesterol, blood pressure, and other standards for maintaining health, we've been determining what students should know and be able to do at a particular grade level. That's the efficient way of expressing the process. Learning and thinking are difficult to quantify, even though we need targets. Learning is not time-dependent, nor is it grade level-dependent. It is human-dependent. An individual student's learning levels are highly variable, but we still expect to see growth and sophistication over time.

When we distill this discussion into an action plan we get the hack: Upgrade the verb. Look for opportunities to elevate those skills the standards define and leverage higher levels of thinking and application than the standards advocate. These skills should extend or unpack the standards' verbs. Armed with unpacked standards, teachers can get to the root of skill expectations fairly quickly and translate the standards into meaningful instructional practices.

Teachers are the learning leaders of their classrooms. It is imperative that they understand how standards translate into skill development and instructional activities, and determine how they will assess the skills they teach. Changing the standards' verbs will help us get down to the real business of teaching for success, no matter the assessment.

WHAT YOU CAN DO TOMORROW

- **"Bloom" where you are.** Think back to your days as a pre-service teacher and what you learned about instructional design. You likely learned about traditional lesson and unit planning, and while those methods are still stalwarts of our design thinking, it's important to dig a little into some of the theoretical bases to determine why those procedures are important. The easiest thing to do here is to remember your past learning about Bloom's Taxonomy (or Webb's Depth of Knowledge or Costa's Thinking Levels). Students need to demonstrate divergent ways of thinking, from low-level recall to high-level evaluation and creativity. Look at tomorrow's plan. Where does divergent thinking fit in? How are students challenged to think on multiple levels?

- **Level up**. Once you consider how different types of thinking will affect learning, move your intentions up a level. For instance, students must often identify characters or describe character traits when they read stories. The verbs for grade levels K-4 in Literature Standard 3 are *identify* and *describe*. For grade 5, the verbs shift to *compare* and *contrast*. As students get older, the verb becomes *analyze*. From K-4, there's not much sophistication in thinking, although there is some sophistication possible if you extend what types of information students identify and describe. By the time 12th grade rolls around, the standard lands on analysis, topping out (at least for this standard) at mid-level thinking. A vendor is going to stick to the language of the standard to inform their instructional design, but a teacher can make better instructional decisions. Teachers will find many opportunities to elevate students' thinking by upgrading a standard's verb, even if it's just one thinking level. Surely, being able to identify and describe characters and their traits is important, but when students can *explain* that importance and *apply* that knowledge to analyze plot structure they have a richer experience with the text.

  Note that this progression of verbs is specific to this standard and that these verbs come up in different ways at different times in other standards. I'm analyzing just this one standard to explain how a teacher might diverge from this standard's thinking levels.

A BLUEPRINT FOR FULL IMPLEMENTATION

Step 1: Understand the sophistication in a year's worth of learning.

As the instructional year unfolds, moving students through the curriculum can challenge teachers in a few different ways. Certainly, building content knowledge is important, but so is guiding students to engage in more sophisticated cognition. Gradually releasing responsibility so a student may reach independent proficiency presents another challenge. Marching through the curriculum like a field-weary soldier does not a learner make. Students have to own the concepts, the thinking, the analysis, the application, and the evaluation. In order for learning to stick the way we intend, we have to be mindful of content *and* cognition.

Step 2: Be cognizant of vertical alignment.

When you compare the same standard from several different grade levels, the increasing sophistication of verbs is apparent. As students progress, the thinking they must do around the content and skills climbs further and further up the Bloom's ladder. Because of this sequence of cognitive sophistication, I often tell teachers that they should be aware of the expectations one grade below and one grade above their current grade level. If teachers aren't too overwhelmed with that prospect, they could familiarize themselves with two grade levels up and down, just to situate their perspective on where their students are coming from and where they need to go. This knowledge is particularly helpful when upping the Bloom's ante over the course of the year.

Step 3: Reflect on your practice.

This change of verbs doesn't come without a caveat. I already know that what I'm suggesting is a cerebral and involved task, but it's extraordinarily worthwhile, particularly if you are documenting your curriculum for comparative analysis to assessment data. That documentation must include reflection. As you engage students in the deeper and more sophisticated skills associated with the verbs you're using in skill statements, note what actually happens in the classroom. Ask questions:

- What did you try and what was the result?
- Was the result expected or unexpected?
- Did roadblocks or opportunities arise?
- How might you change this lesson the next time you try it?
- Was the outcome worth the effort expended on it?
- What was the level of quality in the student products, responses, or other demonstrations of learning?

Record the answers to these questions and revise your documented curriculum accordingly. This keeps your curriculum fresh and alive and provides your students with steadily evolving instructional improvements.

Step 4: Consult your colleagues.

Teachers should never make curricular and instructional decisions alone, particularly those who teach the same content as others on a grade level teacher team. For the sake of instructional equity across your program and everyone's professional growth, collaborate when you tackle verb changes and associated actions, including upgrading skills, instructional activities, and assessments. Perspectives matter here, and so does consensus about curricular decisions.

OVERCOMING PUSHBACK

This requires a lot of planning and PD. Yes, it does. Our students' education is important—it's worth devoting time and resources to ensure success. When all of this hoopla around the Common Core began, remember that the whole initiative was called Race to the Top. One of the huge glaring problems with that name was that many schools took the term "race" seriously and implemented all of the new standards and curricula as quickly as possible. I have to ask, who's winning that race right now: Those who jumped aboard the train and stoked its engines, or those who took things one purposeful step at a time?

Five years into the Common Core initiative, some schools are consistently high performing, awe-inspiring at engagement, and aligned to the Common Core Standards. What are they doing differently than struggling schools? They are investing in their teachers, their communities, and their students. They are ensuring that everyone has the information they need. Their teachers are upgrading teaching skills to have the biggest impact on student learning. In short, they spent the early part of their "race" cultivating vision and culture rather than vendors and politicians. That investment pays off, but only with continued professional development and planning.

If we work beyond grade-level expectations, does that throw off the next year's teacher? This is where collaboration and communication matter so much. It's important for teachers to understand grade-level expectations above and below their current grades. It's even more important for teachers to have discussions with other teachers about the curriculum and the learning outcomes across the system. If a teacher wants to "level up" the verbs in the standards, a conversation with teachers from the next grade will help to determine the best way to pull students forward without encroaching on someone else's territory. Ask them which aspect of the standard is more sophisticated in the next grade: the content or the cognition. It is in the best interest of the teacher to prepare the students so well for the next grade level that state assessments are merely a drop in the bucket of expectations, not the minimum goal. We want students who are capable in any situation, not just during assessments. Work toward total knowledge and skill ownership. The kids benefit when we give them opportunities to grow beyond the standard.

THE HACK IN ACTION

One of my earliest professional development workshops with teachers involved a group of middle grades science teachers in a district in Virginia. This was the first time these fifth through eighth grade teachers had met together as a multi-grade-level group. The objective of the day was to introduce the new curriculum mapping software that their district had purchased and to orient them to the system so that they could document their curriculum. Note that Virginia is not a Common Core state.

We spent most of the morning learning the software, and after lunch the teachers felt that they were ready to start putting some of their work into the system. Two of the grades began by mapping out a beginning of the year unit and the other two grades mapped a unit without committing to a particular time of year. I walked around the room and sat with teams to answer questions and coach them through roadblocks.

When I sat down with the fifth grade team, we discussed their cell unit and its culminating science project. In this time before the proliferation of digital technology, these teachers had developed a typical traditional project. Students were to create a 3D model of an animal or plant cell, complete with all of the internal structures and label it accordingly. The fifth grade teachers recorded the parameters of the project in the curriculum mapping software and went back to work on the other elements of this cell unit.

I moved over to the eighth grade team and discovered that they did not teach physical science exclusively, but multiple areas of science, including life science and earth science. I asked the room if this was the case across grades 5-8 and the teachers confirmed that it was. This was due to the resource that they were using, which taught general overviews of different areas of science in each of the middle school grades, and then students could choose individual scientific disciplines in high school.

As the conversation continued, I discovered that the eighth grade also had a project on cells. Although they weren't mapping the cell unit, I still wanted to know about their version of the project. The teachers explained that students were expected to build a 3D model of a cell with all of the internal structures and to label it correctly. Hmmm. When the eighth grade said this out loud, the seventh grade teachers confirmed that they *also* did a similar cell project. We all turned to the sixth grade, who said that they worked on cells but that there was no project. In sixth grade, students had only to color and label a teacher-supplied diagram.

This was a significant discovery: Four grade levels taught and assessed the same basic topic. We had uncovered an abundance of opportunities. Note that these opportunities wouldn't have come to light if the four grade levels had not come together to work.

We ended up stopping the curriculum mapping for a bit so the whole group could discuss how to teach about cells. Teachers analyzed their curriculum materials and we looked at their standards and the content. While each of the publisher's resources had similar information on cells, each grade level expanded on the content in an increasingly sophisticated way, from describing cell structures to describing cell processes to extensions for cellular interactions and multicellular functions, including cell division in different types of cells. Over the course of four years students should have been progressing through the *what*, the *how*, and the *why* of cells and the way cells work.

Each of these science teachers was only addressing the *what*. By discussing, analyzing resources, and considering more sophisticated skills and instructional practices, the teachers redesigned the cell projects for all four grades while they were together. Each new project had students demonstrate both enhanced content knowledge and deeper thinking.

Teachers documented the new assessments in the mapping software, prompting immediate revisions to skills and instructional activities in the element boxes for this unit. In those skill element boxes, the fifth and sixth grade targeted verbs like *identify, label, recognize, define, explore,* and *explain.* The new seventh and eighth grade maps reflected verbs like *distinguish, predict, support, develop, formulate,* and *propose.* This revision indicated the teachers' thoughtful reflections about higher learning, deeper thinking, and more engagement.

Increasing sophisticated thinking is the mainstay of the Common Core. When students can think more deeply and problem solve independently, they are better prepared for the next grade level. By moving the standards' verbs up levels in Bloom's Taxonomy, teachers can effectively prepare students for deeper learning, better performance, and overall readiness for college and careers.

HACK 9

ONE SIZE FITS NONE

Adapt to fit every learner

If my future were determined just by my performance on a standardized test, I wouldn't be here. I guarantee you that.
—MICHELLE OBAMA, FIRST LADY

THE PROBLEM: NEW ASSESSMENTS AREN'T GIVING US GOOD DATA

EDUCATION IS EVOLVING, and not necessarily in a positive way. In misguided attempts to quantify every little thing and compare massive amounts of data as if school were an exercise in extreme business planning techniques, we're missing the primary reason we're in business: the customer. The student.

The proponents of the business model would have us believe that it is possible to quantify learning accurately with one high-stakes assessment that measures year-to-year growth, how well a teacher teaches, and whether the school is effective. The number of variables presents a problem here. Scientific experiments adjust one variable at a time, an approach that allows a scientist to categorize the possible outcomes before drawing conclusions based on comparative observation. Our current multivariable model does not sort out individual variables from outcomes before drawing conclusions. This not only amounts to bad science, but it leads to bad practices.

I'm not saying that assessment is bad. Valid assessment measures our success: Why in the world would we practice for a game we never will play or rehearse for a performance we never will present? Of course the system requires checks and balances to ensure that students succeed. But the system also needs integrity. That integrity must be founded in our fundamental priority: Keep the learner at the center. Focusing on the good of the student means that we must find more rational ways to assess—it's disgraceful that assessment is causing complete psychological breakdowns on test days. Any worthwhile system of assessment must also address the variables that the current system keeps in the periphery, such as poverty, family and environmental support, and equity and fairness in instructional practices.

Raising test scores is not our objective. Teaching children is our objective.

THE HACK: GO BEYOND ONE-SIZE-FITS-ALL

In the past two decades we've improved curriculum and instruction significantly with many exciting ways to teach and learn and myriad ways to access media. But what has changed about standardized assessment? Not a single thing. Even though teachers have been led to think that outcomes of standardized assessment are their sole responsibility, they cannot be held at fault for the system's antiquated methods. Outside of the standardized assessments ensconced in schools around the country, teachers have myriad methods to assess students in dynamic and divergent ways. It's just hard to assess in dynamic and divergent ways and still have consistency and validity across hundreds of schools across the country. It's also difficult to compare assessment results across those hundreds of schools if the metrics are all different. So we're left with standardization: a very sanitized version of assessment that creates the illusion of progress and a misaligned objective of raising test scores.

Raising test scores is not our objective. Teaching children is our objective.

We don't want automatons in the classroom checking off to-do lists to make sure we've covered as much land as possible before the assessment. That's not what the Common Core advocates. The Common Core, in its most drilled-down state, promotes deeper thinking. Deeper thinking doesn't happen when we're so worried about "the test" that we feel the need to adhere with fidelity to a vendor's or politician's views about how to raise test scores.

The essence of this hack is simply extraordinary teaching. Teach children to go deep and justify their thinking as often as possible. Teach them to question and explore and really learn what's worth learning, not just what's easy to measure. Ask students "Why?" as often as possible and listen to their answers. Get back to risk taking and making learning magic.

WHAT YOU CAN DO TOMORROW

- **Stop the test prep.** Or at least stop shutting down instruction to take a bunch of practice tests in the weeks leading up to a big assessment. Embed test-taking skills throughout the school year and occasionally practice learning opportunities that require stamina and endurance, such as working on research or solving involved multistep equations.

- **Build relationships.** Content matters, but caring matters a whole lot more. Do everything you possibly can to build relationships with students, regardless of their age, so that they believe that you are on their team. Likewise, reach out to homes and families and participate in community activities. Learning is so much easier when students feel supported and safe. You might be the only one that treats them that way.

- **Stop having students pulled out of class during learning time.** Now before anyone gets upset at this statement, I'm not saying to stop pulling kids out of class altogether, particularly if they need the additional support. What I'm suggesting here is to keep them in class for new learning or essential guided learning. I also realize that scheduling conflicts and other classes like physical education, library, music, and art play a role, but make sure that you're scheduling for student success rather than adult convenience. Better times to pull students out of class would be when they are working on skill development or independent practice, particularly if the support classes focus on scaffolded and individualized instruction of skills and independent practice.

A BLUEPRINT FOR FULL IMPLEMENTATION

Step 1: Teach beyond the assessment.

Now that we've had at least a couple of years of new Common Core assessments, we have more information about what's on them. Use whatever it is that you know about them as a baseline for non-negotiable proficiencies throughout the year. Get students up to speed with instructional scaffolds as necessary if you recognize any deficits, and then forge ahead. I don't mean you should try to get through all of your

Common Core curriculum before the test, I mean make strategic adaptations to your curriculum so that students are both building a solid foundation of content knowledge and thinking in depth. Adaptations could include exploring, researching, asking and refining questions, researching again, creating, evaluating, and discovering.

Step 2: Less doing, more learning.

It amazes me that when I walk into classrooms and ask students about what they are doing and what they are learning, I still get two very different reactions. Students can tell me step-by-step directions for what they are doing. When I ask them what they are learning, they falter. They aren't sure. Many students see school as a place to do things, but not necessarily as a place to learn. We need to change that by giving them opportunities to truly learn, to dig deeply into new ideas the way explorers investigate unfamiliar lands. Students should acquire "scientist personas" that they can adopt for every class, regardless of content; identities that drive them to question, gather data, draw conclusions, and defend those conclusions.

> **Reading, writing, speaking, and listening need to be focal points for every educator, regardless of content area.**

Step 3: Engage in rich conversations.

Put down the worksheet and talk to the students. To create from their learning, students must have internalized what they've studied. The ways in which they receive new learning influence their ability to take ownership of it. Therefore, we have to engage in receptive teaching and learning behaviors with students. Having meaningful Socratic discussions engages that receptive capacity so that when it's time for the students to be expressive, they can genuinely do so.

Step 4: Offer enrichment opportunities.

For the sake of equity, give students the gift of differentiated experiences, even if this is just providing access to computers and books before or after the school day. Access to resources has a profound effect on student learning, and the disparity for those who have no access is 100 percent a social justice issue. The more exposure students have to multiple perspectives, multiple types of media, and other enriching experiences, the more likely they are to do well on assessments and move on to higher education. Let's give them that opportunity.

Step 5: Support literacy in every nook and cranny.

A great way to support teaching beyond the assessment is to make sure that every single person on a school's staff is on board with literacy. Reading, writing, speaking, and listening need to be focal points for every educator, regardless of content area. All teachers can ask students to make inferences and draw conclusions about whatever learning is happening in their classrooms. Enhancing every student's literacy is of paramount importance. It gives them entry into texts and media that they might not otherwise have had access to. Give them that gift.

OVERCOMING PUSHBACK

How do you rise above the assessment when no one is near grade level? You can't go in with a defeatist attitude, that's for sure. These children are depending on you. Figure out the priorities in instruction and create an action plan. Begin with a few questions:

- Are their deficits mainly foundational?

- Are they inconsistent performers?

- Do they have generalized misconceptions that need re-teaching?

- Are they disengaged?

Work to design learning experiences rather than lesson plans that isolate content. Create opportunities for students to integrate thinking, evaluation, making decisions, providing evidence for thinking, engaging powerful vocabulary, and building independence with content knowledge proficiency. Give students the time to genuinely process information so that your classes are geared toward depth of learning rather than coverage of content.

How will I get grades for conversations, enrichment, and high expectations? Something has to go home on the report card. Let rubrics be your friend and begin thinking about standards-based reporting rather than traditional grades. Report cards should report where students are as learners rather than being an opportunity to exalt or damn them with meaningless letters and numbers that more often than not still reflect behavioral elements rather than actual quantified learning.

This is impossible. My teacher evaluation score depends on that end-of-year assessment score. What a sad state of affairs we're in. I'm so sorry that many educators are in this position. I'm embarrassed for politicians whose agendas and opinions about education are so skewed that they make decisions that are detrimental to the entire system. The biggest weapon you have in your arsenal to combat this ridiculous situation is your professional awesomeness. Investing in our own profession has dividends that transcend tests. If you're constantly improving, then greater gains on assessments are likely byproducts. We need to make the standardized measure only a small slice of our academic worries rather than a year-long focus. Each of us needs to be at our best all the time.

THE HACK IN ACTION

The information I've offered in this hack arises out of my personal experiences in classrooms. As I've worked with schools around the country, I have observed many teachers, and by examining their practices and conversing with them, I've learned a great deal about intentional and effective practices.

Some of the teachers that I've worked with consistently perform highly on standardized tests, even though their objective is not necessarily improvement on those standardized tests. I thought it would be important to share some common facets of their practices, which include:

- Collaborative cultures are an integral part of their work. Teachers work together and have at least weekly conversations about curriculum and student concerns.

- These teachers know their standards explicitly.

- The teachers have high levels of the qualities Andy Hargreaves and Michael Fullan note in their work about commitment and capabilities. These teachers are deeply committed and highly capable in all facets of their professional actions.

- They design their own curriculum. While the curriculum may include vendor products, it never relies on them.

- Their classrooms contain a high degree of joy in teaching and learning.

- The children in their classes are excited about learning.

- These teachers have good rapport with their colleagues and the community, including the parents of their students. In fact, parents often come in to help in many of these high-performing classrooms.

- There are a lot of projects going on. Students in these classrooms are often working collaboratively on projects or authentic problems to solve.

Excellence in teaching matters. Don't let the system get you down. Keep being excellent.

Standardized testing is endemic in our current system. We don't have a choice about it happening, but we do have a choice in how we think about it. If we are preparing students so well that the state or vendor assessments are just blips, then we remove anxiety about the assessment. We have to remember to focus on our students, not these assessments. Teacher performance, grades, graduation, and student intervention services should not hang on one standardized test.

INVOLVE PARENTS

Clarify their role

I do not think it means what you think it means.
—INIGO MONTOYA, FICTIONAL AVENGER

THE PROBLEM: PARENTS DON'T UNDERSTAND THEIR ROLE

WHILE THE COMMON Core has brought its share of heartache to America's teachers, it's been equally frustrating for parents. What started with good conversations about new standards and curriculum quickly devolved into "us and them" policy conversations and organizing to opt out of standardized testing.

While standards-based instruction has been around for more than forty years, social media hasn't. With new tools like Twitter and Facebook, parents have found efficient and convenient ways to communicate their opinions about the standards, schools, evaluations, and assessments. Some of the information has been accurate, but much of it has deteriorated into hearsay, conspiracy theories, and widespread misinformation.

THE HACK: MAKE SURE PARENTS UNDERSTAND THEIR ROLE

This hack is a little different than all of the previous hacks. This hack is about the "Outside-In" approach rather than an "Inside-Out" approach. Parents need to know what their responsibilities are. They need to focus on what's best for kids, their kids *and* other people's kids.

The system has an obligation to get this right, but for this to happen all of the pieces of the system have to work.

For parents to buy into your programs and curricular decisions, they need to be aware of them in multifaceted ways.

Parents and students are components in the system, as are teachers, administrators, policy makers, even voters and businesses. Everyone needs a seat at the table. My colleague, Marie Alcock of Learning Systems Associates, calls this having a *culture of connection* rather than a *culture of correction*.

If we were to focus on students and preparing them for the future, consider what would change in terms of our conversations. Perhaps our essential questions would center on invitation and collaboration. Perhaps instead of identifying roadblocks, we could figure out how to move past them.

WHAT YOU CAN DO TOMORROW

Note that the following are generalizations not specific to Common Core or its implementation—they are just good practices for inviting the community, and specifically parents, into the conversation.

- **Believe that parents are on your team**. This is non-negotiable. Every educational organization must figure out how to engage parents. Schools need to invite parent participation in a multitude of ways: parent nights, curriculum meetings, dinner meetings, Parent Teacher Association events, whatever it takes.

- **Become a customer service specialist.** Call ten parents. Do this as often as possible. Call with an invitation, a positive comment, or a personal observation about their child. Surely you can call for other reasons as well, but putting effort into positive experiences will pay big dividends. When I was in the classroom, I had a "1 to 3" policy. If I had to make a negative phone call home or have an unpleasant discussion with parents about their child, then I made three positive phone calls immediately after. Also, when I did have to make a negative phone call, I always found something positive to say even if I was beyond frustrated.

- **Share your work.** Transparency is a must-do. Begin adding material to the school website, not only to share fun happenings, but also to show curriculum documents and student-created work. For parents to buy into your programs and curricular decisions, they need to be aware of them in multifaceted ways. Share successes. When students do something outstanding, share, share, share!

- **Model the behaviors you desire.** Administrators should model collaborative behaviors with the community at large the way they want their teachers to collaborate with parents. Collaboration with communities and families should be a given in a school's mission and culture.

A BLUEPRINT FOR FULL IMPLEMENTATION

Step 1: Invite parents into the Common Core conversation.

Assuage fears by sharing jargon-free information every time parents are in the school. Plan events multiple times throughout the school year to share information about standards, curriculum, and assessment, and conduct panel discussions and question/answer sessions. Make sure teachers are communicating expectations for student proficiencies using the language of the skills in the standards and conveying how the curriculum helps students to become more sophisticated learners. Clarify any concerns or questions the parents have.

Step 2: Choose to appreciate whatever is offered.

We need to meet parents where they are. Be mindful that not all parents had positive experiences in school and that might leave them wary of the way things work now. Anything they are able to offer—showing up for a teacher meeting, participating in a school-wide event, joining the Parent Teacher Association, speaking at a board meeting, whatever it is—sincerely appreciate it and make that parent feel like royalty for contributing to the betterment of the school. Sometimes all that people can offer is a kind word. Take whatever you can get and celebrate it. Celebrating it invites opportunities for more interactions.

Step 3: Leverage social media.

To be honest, I think that social media was a major catalyst for the current opt-out movement, and it's a rallying point for the collective anger of anything related to the Common Core. We've had standards-based instruction and standardized testing for decades, but it's only since the prevalence of digital communication that the general public has entered so vehemently into the conversation about them. Sure, these last few years have seen the addition of ridiculous teacher evaluations based on the scores, ineffective remediation based on narrow assessments, and frustrated students who have been ill-prepared to meet the challenge of the assessments. This certainly accounts in some degree for the upsurge of discourse about standards in the community.

The conversation online does not have to be so predominantly negative. Social media can be an opportunity for better communication. Rather than conducting emotionally charged rants, we can talk about sharing solutions and effective dialogue between stakeholders. Dirty laundry should stay in the laundry basket and not be aired on social media. Our objective is improved student learning, even amidst the political sludge through which we all must wade. We must move forward together, which necessitates using social media for dialogue, shared (accurate) information, and community building. What we do together carries weight, and social media can be a great tool to amplify the community.

Step 4: Make sure the parents understand their role in the English language arts shifts.

The instructional shifts are not just about teacher actions in the classroom. They are really meant to be applied across the board by all stakeholders, students and parents included. We want to create opportunities for students to access more sophisticated learning, and to do that we need a collaborative culture of teaching and learning that extends well beyond the school walls. In language arts, this means parents help their children to find and experience multiple types of texts and have conversations about what their children are reading. Parents should model good reading habits and expect their children to read often at home. Likewise, parents and children should read together. Parents should ask their children questions that require them to provide textual evidence to support their claims or explanations. They should encourage their children to write and help them use digital tools to do so. And most important, parents need to expose children as early as possible to sophisticated vocabulary. They should use increasingly complex words and expect their children to use those words when they speak.

Step 5: Show parents how to help with the shifts in math.

There's been significant parental pushback to the new curricular materials for the Common Core math standards. The instructional shifts associated with math advocate for doing things differently than the way we learned math as kids. Some of the vendors who created curriculum for schools interpreted those standards in strange and divergent ways. The whole point of the Common Core in math is conceptual level knowledge rather than rote remembering. Students might be able to remember a trick to solve a problem, but anything outside of that trick zone is out of their thinking bounds because they don't truly understand the concept or process. Parents should be seeing more opportunities for depth rather than breadth in their child's schoolwork. Rather than doing numerous problems, children should be focusing on a few more sophisticated problems. Parents can help their children be better at conceptual-level learning by engaging their children in a few but important strategies. Have children practice fluency, which involves adding and subtracting small numbers and knowing multiplication with some level of automaticity. Parents can support their children with authentic, real-world math by asking their children about math related to their environment, such as prices on items at the grocery store, time it would take to get to your destination if you travel X distance at different speeds, problem-solving a home improvement task like hanging a set of pictures on the wall. Also worth mentioning is that the Common Core is about *divergence* in thinking, not just thinking the way the vendor or teacher is teaching. Students need multiple ways to solve problems, not just a predictable way.

OVERCOMING PUSHBACK

The Common Core is dictating too much curriculum. In many places it is, but understand that the standards and the curriculum are two different things. The standards inform the curriculum. The Common

Core is a set of standards, separated by grade level, that give stakeholders a benchmark idea of what a student should know and be able to do. The curriculum articulates the skills, activities, and assessments that will allow students to meet the standards. One is not the other. So, in actuality, it is the curriculum rather than the Common Core that dictates instructional practice. Personally, I advocate for teachers, in teams, to create a curriculum based on whatever standards they are using (Common Core or otherwise) that reflect their student population.

We don't see this as preparing our kids for the real world. Even before the Common Core, colleges were reporting that students are ill-prepared to meet the rigors (vigors!) of college-level work. Likewise, business leaders tell us that recent graduates may be full of content knowledge, but they don't do so well with solving unique problems, being perseverant, and working with others toward a common goal. Students can't "Think, Pair, Share" their way to successful creative problem solving in a job setting. Take a look at two documents that are critical to effective implementation and alignment of the Common Core Standards: The College and Career Readiness Capacities and the Standards for Mathematical Practice. These outline some umbrella facets of the contemporary learner. In the ELA document, these facets include descriptors such as building content knowledge, thinking critically, and inviting global perspectives. In math, they include being able to construct viable arguments, reason abstractly, look for patterns, and be precise. There's much more information in each of these documents stakeholders should know and use to work with students. Every single Common Core Standard relates back to at least one of these capacities or practices in some way.

These tests are insane, developmentally inappropriate, and/or hurting my child. This one is going to take some communication. Standardized tests, to paraphrase Art Costa, measure what is easy to measure but not necessarily what is worth measuring. There are several factors at work here. One is the range of the children that will be tested. In many states, Departments of Assessment are responsible for testing more than a million students. In order for them to be as reliable and valid as possible, all students take the same test under the same conditions in the same window of time. These assessments, even the ones perceived as evil or inappropriate, still give schools information about their instructional program. Sometimes questions from these assessments pop up on Facebook or Twitter and parents and the community lament their inappropriateness or the new level of challenge and it stirs everyone up. One of the things that you should know is that humans make these tests and there likely are some errors. Sometimes vendors vet them through a lens that has more to do with their products than with the standards themselves. There are also things to know about text complexity and conceptual-level knowledge related to the tests. These assessments do give schools information beyond just content. Schools get information about a student's response/proficiency with different types of questions and different cognitive levels of the question, which inform instructional programs. That said, parents should still ask questions. If they are uncomfortable, they should speak up. If something doesn't look right to them or they really feel like their child is needlessly suffering, then they should communicate those thoughts and feelings. We all have a responsibility to get this as right as we can and we all must be at the table to solve problems and forge ahead.

THE HACK IN ACTION

A large school district in Western New York hired a new superintendent a couple of years after the statewide implementation of the Common Core had begun. This superintendent spoke with all stakeholders, including parents and students, as soon as she took the position, and realized that the previous administration had given parents very little information about the Common Core Standards and the new assessments.

In her previous district, this superintendent had been well known for rallying the community and having a vision and culture that were supported by everyone. She was also a straight shooter, a tell-it-like-it-is type who spoke in words that the whole audience of stakeholders could understand, with little educational jargon. She discovered that the community in her current district had not really been an active one in the past and it was her mission to change that, not because of Common Core, but because it is what is best for kids. She had a strong belief that when everyone is involved, then everyone benefits from overlapping expertise and perspective.

She convened her administrative team and they planned to create a series of parent nights, which would be part informational, part question and answer, and part fellowship. In the past, the administrators said that they had had some luck with attendance at parent events when they served food. So, each of the four planned parent nights was to include dinner or desserts. One of the elementary administrators suggested that they have a room dedicated to child-care so that the events would be accessible by all families.

The team advertised these nights with take-home fliers and on the school's social media. On each of the nights, the schedule consisted of food and fellowship, a few concurrent sessions about issues that mattered to the parents, the topics of which came from informal feedback as well as surveys. Each of the nights was capped with a question-and-answer period where parents could safely share concerns and converse with administrators and teachers.

This was not without its roadblocks. Attendance at the first two sessions was lower than it was at the final two sessions, but the district saw an improvement over time, particularly in light of the limited parent involvement in previous years. Another issue was dealing with emotions. Some parents were very upset about the new standards, new curricula, and new assessments, but through conversation, the administrators and teachers discovered that there was much misinformation being shared, particularly by the local media, who tended to sensationalize dramatic bits of information.

I don't want to paint too rosy a picture here. Things are not perfect in this district, but they are better. The community is committed to continued conversation, and right now that's enough. There are still concerns about new curricula and new assessments, and the school district is trying to be as transparent as possible while still making sure they do what is necessary according to state education law. They are weathering frustrations and successes together, and I think that's about the best scenario that they can have.

Parents must be part of the conversation. Inviting them into the Common Core conversation brings them onto the instructional team and allows them to better help their children at home. When everyone's at the table, children benefit.

CONCLUSION

*Liberating education consists of acts of
cognition, not transferals of information.*
—Paulo Freire, Educational Theorist

I HOPE THAT *HACKING the Common Core* has given you some ideas, some goals perhaps, to hack your classroom intentions. I also hope those intentions include collegial conversation and collaboration so that you and your curriculum team can develop your own interpretation of what the standards mean and determine how to translate your ideas into instructional actions.

You'll find it easier to meet your goal if you construct a series of steps to get there and define specific ways to show that you have succeeded. Many of us rely on a GPS to plan our paths and target our destinations when we navigate journeys in our modern world. I often use the acronym GPS with teachers when I ask them to think about their curriculum destinations. Set *Goals*, create intentional steps in the *Process*, and define *Success*. Consider your own goals, processes, and successes. Which new curricular paths and destinations might you travel to when you think of your own GPS?

Hack the Common Core in your classroom by setting goals centered on ideas you have observed or read about that you want to implement or upgrade. Figure out which hacks you might incorporate to have a positive impact on student learning, your professional practice, or collegial dialogue. Think about how what you have read here might inform instruction in analysis or vocabulary processes. In short, decide what you want to accomplish and express it as a goal or series of goals.

Creating a process means setting a course of intentional actions to get you to your goal. Some potential questions to ask as you chart out this series of steps are: What kind of foundation needs to be laid in order for me to do this work? Who will I need on my team to help with the implementation? What kinds of resources will I need? Where will I find the time to make this happen? What are some specific actions I can record to help keep me accountable to my intentions?

Success is multi layered. You may certainly think of success in terms of what kinds of validation might represent meeting your goal(s). It should also take the form of defined products or outcomes. However, take the time to be creative and think about success as a series of "what if" possibilities. What if everything fell into place and you did something more remarkable than you were planning? What would that look like? Would that be worth aspiring to?

The Common Core Standards reflect the *science* of teaching, not its *art*. This does not mean that the art of teaching gets shunted aside: Now that the standards have been clearly defined, teachers can use them to inform the art, the content and skills of actual classroom work. Common Core allows for design decisions based on the *science*, outlining vigorous standards with higher expectations. It should help states to find a common ground so that no matter where in our country a child goes to school, he or she will get a more consistent experience based on the content and skills from the standards. Consistency doesn't mean that all states are going to be required to use M&Ms for counting practice, or that everyone must study Marxism as a critical lens in September, even if that's what critics would have you believe.

The Common Core Standards are an opportunity for teachers to appraise their current classroom practices and professional interactions. Teachers should be considering how they can become more contemporary in practice, whether these standards are the impetus for change or not. We do *not* want a Race to Mediocrity, nor do we want a nation of compliance.

Teachers need to talk to each other, to their students, to their administrators, to the parents. Purposeful curriculum design and collegial, consensual curriculum conversations are the direction we need to be heading. If the stakeholders can agree to some critical pieces, then we can start building equity in instruction, and we thus can reach our intended curricular goals. The whole system needs to change, to grow, to bloom. Change is challenging, yes, but we can attain what we intend, moving well beyond our aspirations. Our students deserve to be college- and career-ready. They deserve to not be limited by our experiences. They deserve to be prepared for their world. When we hack the Common Core, we open that world up to them.

OTHER BOOKS IN THE
HACK LEARNING SERIES

HACKING EDUCATION
10 Quick Fixes For Every School

By Mark Barnes (@markbarnes19) & Jennifer Gonzalez (@cultofpedagogy)

In the bestselling *Hacking Education*, Mark Barnes and Jennifer Gonzalez employ decades of teaching experience and hundreds of discussions with education thought leaders, to show you how to find and hone the quick fixes that every school and classroom need. Using a Hacker's mentality, they provide one Aha moment after another with 10 Quick Fixes For Every School—solutions to everyday problems and teaching methods that any teacher or administrator can implement immediately.

"Barnes and Gonzalez don't just solve problems; they turn teachers into hackers—a transformation that is right on time."
— DON WETTRICK, AUTHOR OF *PURE GENIUS*

MAKE WRITING
5 Teaching Strategies That Turn Writers Workshop Into a Maker Space

By Angela Stockman (@angelastockman)

Everyone's favorite education blogger and writing coach, Angela Stockman, turns teaching strategies and practice upside down in the bestseller, *Make Writing*. She spills you out of your chair, shreds your lined paper, and launches you and your writer's workshop into the maker space! Stockman provides five right-now writing strategies that reinvent instruction and inspire both young and adult writers to express ideas with tools and in ways that have rarely, if ever, been considered. Make Writing is a fast-paced journey inside Stockman's Western New York Young Writer's Studio, alongside the students there who learn how to write and how to make, employing Stockman's unique teaching methods.

HACKING ASSESSMENT
10 Ways to Go Gradeless in a Traditional Grades School

By Starr Sackstein (@mssackstein)

In the bestselling *Hacking Assessment,* award-winning teacher and world-renowned formative assessment expert Starr Sackstein unravels one of education's oldest mysteries: How to assess learning without grades—even in a school that uses numbers, letters, GPAs, and report cards. While many educators can only muse about the possibility of a world without grades, teachers like Sackstein are reimagining education. In this unique, eagerly-anticipated book, Sackstein shows you exactly how to create a remarkable no-grades classroom like hers, a vibrant place where students grow, share, thrive, and become independent learners who never ask, "What's this worth?"

RESOURCES TO HELP YOU HACK LEARNING

Hack Learning Series information:
http://hacklearningseries.com

The Hack Learning Academy:
http://hacklearningacademy.com

Hack Learning on Facebook:
https://www.facebook.com/groups/hacklearningteam/

The Hack Learning Store:
http://hacklearningstore.com

Hack Learning on Pinterest:
https://www.pinterest.com/hacklearning/

Hack Learning on Twitter:
#HackLearning

ABOUT THE AUTHOR

 Michael Fisher is an instructional coach and educational consultant specializing in the intersection between instructional technology and curriculum design. He works with districts across the country helping teachers and schools maximize available technology, software, and Web-based resources while attending to curriculum design, instructional practices, and assessments. He posts frequently at ASCD Edge (edge.ascd.org), the Curriculum 21 blog (www.curriculum21.com/blog), and his own blog (digigogy.blogspot.com). He's written several books on curriculum and technology, including *Ditch the Daily Lesson Plan*, *Upgrade Your Curriculum: Practical Ways to Transform Units and Engage Students* with co-author Janet Hale, and *Digital Learning Strategies: How Do I Assign and Assess 21st Century Work?* He's also a contributing author to the Solution Tree Series *Contemporary Perspectives on Literacy*. You can contact him via Twitter @fisher1000 or by visiting his website at www.digigogy.com.

PUBLICATIONS

Times 10 is helping all education stakeholders improve every aspect of teaching and learning. We are committed to solving big problems with simple ideas. We bring you content from experts, shared through multiple channels, including books, video courses, webinars, and an array of social networks. Our mantra is simple: Read it today; fix it tomorrow.

Lightning Source UK Ltd.
Milton Keynes UK
UKOW04f1411110716

278100UK00009B/407/P